The Inner Sky

THE INNER SKY

poems, notes, dreams by

RAINER MARIA RILKE

A BILINGUAL EDITION

selected & translated by Damion Searls

 David R. Godine · Publisher
Boston

First published in 2010 by
DAVID R. GODINE · *Publisher*
Post Office Box 450
Jaffrey, New Hampshire 03452
www.godine.com

The translator is grateful to the U.S. National Endowment for the Arts,
Het beschrijf's writers and translators residency in Vollezele, Belgium, and
the city of Klagenfurt, Austria, for support during the translation of this
book. Special thanks to the novelist, poet, and translator Ulrike Draesner,
who was very generous with her time and intelligence and helped make
these translations both truer and better.

"Interiors" was first published in slightly different form in *The Paris Review*
(Issue 190, Fall 2009), and "Notes on the Melody of Things" in *The Literary
Review* (Fall 2008) and on PEN America's website, *www.pen.org*.

LIBRARY OF CONGRESS
CATALOGING-IN-PUBLICATION DATA

Rilke, Rainer Maria, 1875–1926.
[Selections. English. 2010]
Inner sky : poems, notes, dreams / by Rainer Maria Rilke ;
translated by Damion Searls.
p.   cm.
Includes indexes.
ISBN 978-1-56792-388-9
1. Rilke, Rainer Maria, 1875–1926—Translations into English.
I. Searls, Damion. II. Title.
PT2635.I65A6 2010
831'.912—dc22
2009022393

SECOND PRINTING, 2012
Printed in the United States of America

Contents

"As long as you catch what you've thrown yourself" · 9

Pregnant Woman · 11

Interiors · 13

Young Girl · 31

The Lady and the Unicorn · 33

On Completing the Circle (I–II) · 35

Dedication · 41

Vitali Awoke · 43

Notes on the Melody of Things · 45

Haiku (I–II) · 65

Poems from the Graveyard (I–V) · 67

On the Poet's Material · 75

Marriage · 77

In His Thirty-Eighth Year · 79

From Testament · 83

"Come then, come, you last thing I have learned" · 91

On Shawls and Lemons (I–IV) · 93

"There is total silence..." · 105

From the Notebooks (Naples–Capri–Paris) · 107

Night Songs (I–II) · 115

Note on Birds · 117

Spring Songs (I–II) · 119

"It's not that now that we're (suddenly) grown up" · 121

When Death Came with the Morning · 125

"Looking up from the book, from the near and
    countable lines" · 129

Dream (Fragment) · 131

The Origin of the Chimera · 133

From the Dream-Book (The Seventh, Eleventh,
    and Twenty-Sixth Dreams) · 135

Morning Prayer · 149

"What birds hurtle through is not the familiar sky" · 153

Chronology, Notes, Extras · 155

Translator's Afterword · 171

Envoi: Introduction to a Poetry Reading · 184

Index of English Titles and First Lines · 187

Index of Original Titles and First Lines · 189

The Inner Sky

Solang du Selbstgeworfnes fängst, ist alles
Geschicklichkeit und läßlicher Gewinn–;
erst wenn du plötzlich Fänger wirst des Balles,
den eine ewige Mit-Spielerin
dir zuwarf, deiner Mitte, in genau
gekonntem Schwung, in einem jener Bögen
aus Gottes großem Brücken-Bau:
erst dann ist Fangen-Können ein Vermögen, –
nicht deines, einer Welt. Und wenn du gar
zurückzuwerfen Kraft und Mut besäßest,
nein, wunderbarer: Mut und Kraft vergäßest
und schon geworfen *hättest* . . . (wie das Jahr
die Vögel wirft, die Wandervogelschwärme,
die eine ältre einer jungen Wärme
hinüberschleudert über Meere –) erst
in diesem Wagnis spielst du gültig mit.
Erleichterst dir den Wurf nicht mehr; erschwerst
dir ihn nicht mehr. Aus deinen Händen tritt
das Meteor und rast in seine Räume. . .

As long as you catch what you've thrown yourself, it's all
just clever agility and venial gain;
but when you suddenly come to catch a ball
an eternal playmate has thrown
at you, at your center, has exactly set
in mastered motion, in an arc
out of God's great bridge-building –
then that you can catch is real power:
not yours, the world's. And when you even
have the strength and courage to throw it back,
no, better yet: have forgotten courage and strength
and thrown it back *already* . . . (the way the year
throws birds, the flocks of migrating birds
hurled over the ocean from an old to a new
warmth –) then, that gamble, is the first moment
you too can be said to play. You
unburden yourself of the throw no longer; you burden
yourself with the throw no longer. Out of your hands steps
the meteor and it races into its skies. . .

[Schwangere]

Wehtag, der wie eine Wunde klafft,
hohler wird das Haus von ihrem Heulen,
und sie drängt an alle Porphyrsäulen
aufgerissen ihre Schwangerschaft.
Und sie wirft sich wie ein Innenbrand
aufwärtsschlagend in die Fensternischen
und sie möchte sich mit Haar vermischen
überhängt und unerkannt.
Aber löschte sie sich durch ein Wunder
wirklich unter Haar und Händen aus,
stünde nicht ihr treibender und runder
Leib aus der Unkenntlichkeit hinaus –?

Pregnant Woman

Day of pain that gapes like a wound.
The house grows hollow from her howling.
She presses, torn open, her pregnancy
at all the columns of porphyry.

She hurls herself like inner fire,
upstriking, at the window bays.
She longs for anonymity,
mingled with overhanging hair.

But can she, by some miracle, truly
extinguish herself under hair and hands,
doesn't her round and pushing body
bulge out from the unknown? . . .

Intérieurs

I. Man muß sie gesehen haben, diese kleinen und ganz kleinen Städte in meiner Heimat. Sie haben *einen* Tag auswendig gelernt; den schreien sie immerfort wie große graue Papageien in die Sonne hinein. Nah an der Nacht aber werden sie namenlos nachdenklich. Man sieht es den Plätzen an, daß sie sich bemühen, die dunkle Frage zu lösen, die in der Luft liegt. Das ist rührend und ein wenig lächerlich für den Fremden. Denn er weiß ohneweiters: giebt es eine Antwort – irgendeine –, dann kommt sie bestimmt nicht von den kleinen und ganz kleinen Städten meiner Heimat her, – sie mögen sich noch so ehrlich anstrengen, die Armen.

II. Wenn ich an kleine Mädchen denke, die gerade große Mädchen werden (das ist keine langsame zaghafte Entwickelung, sondern etwas seltsam Plötzliches), so muß ich mir hinter ihnen ein Meer denken, oder eine ernste, ewige Ebene oder sonst etwas, was man eigentlich nicht schauen, sondern nur ahnen kann und auch das nur in stillen, tiefen Stunden. Dann sehe ich die großen Mädchen ebenso groß, als ich die kleinen und kinderhaften winzig gewohnt war; – und weiß der liebe Himmel weshalb ich sie nun einmal so sehen will. Es hat alles seinen Grund. Aber die besten Dinge und Ereignisse sind doch die, welche ihre Ursache mit beiden Händen verdecken, sei es aus Bescheidenheit oder weil sie nicht verraten sein wollen.

III. Aber trotzdem: auch in den kleinen und ganz kleinen Städten meiner Heimat werden die kleinen Mädchen über Nacht große Mädchen. Ich kann es nicht hindern und kann auch nachträglich kein Meer hinter ihrem Rücken ausgießen, weil das zur Folge hätte, daß die jüngeren Brüder, die ihr Zehn-Uhr-Butterbrot noch in der Schule essen, beim Heimkommen erzählen müßten: »Was in der Geographie steht ist falsch. Und der Herr Lehrer hat gelogen. Er hat uns gesagt, daß das Meer tief unten beginnt, ganz am Rand der Landkarte von Österreich-Ungarn. Und nun ist es mitten im Königreich Böhmen – das

Interiors

I. You must have seen them: these small towns and tiny villages of my homeland. They have learned *one day* by heart and they scream it out into the sunlight over and over again like great gray parrots. Near night though they grow preternaturally pensive. You can see it in the town squares, where they struggle to solve the dark question that hangs in the air. It is touching, and a little ludicrous, to the foreigner, because he knows without a second thought that if there is an answer – any answer at all – it certainly won't come from the small towns and tiny villages of my homeland, try as sincerely as they might, poor things.

II. When I think about little girls in the moment of turning into big girls (it is no slow timid development, but something strangely sudden), I always have to imagine an ocean behind them, or a grave eternal plain, or something else you don't actually see with your eyes but can only sense, and that only in the deep and silent hours. Then I see the big girls as being exactly as big as I was used to the little childlike girls being small – and Heaven above knows why, that's just how I want to see them. There is a reason for everything. But the best things that happen, after all, are the ones which hide their deeper reason with both hands, whether out of modesty or because they don't want to be betrayed.

III. Even so: in the small towns and tiny villages of my homeland too the little girls turn into big girls overnight. I cannot prevent it, and I cannot pour out an ocean behind their backs after the fact, because that would mean that their younger brothers, who still eat their ten-o'clock bread and butter at school, would need to tell everyone when they got home: "The geography book is wrong. And our teacher lied. He told us the ocean starts way down at the bottom edge of the map of the Austro-Hungarian Empire. And now it's here in the middle of the Kingdom of Bohemia – the ocean." I know that

Meer.« Und ich weiß, daß die kleinen Klugheiten überlegen lächeln bei solchen Erkenntnissen. Und doch ist das Lächeln über das Meer, das ich unerwartet mitten in Böhmen gemacht habe, lange nicht so licht, wie die Freude, mit welcher sie sich selber angesichts der blanken Dielen oder des Furchenfeldes befehlen: das ist das Meer. So will ich die Schöpfung diesen kleinen Allmächtigen überlassen und mich damit zufrieden geben, daß hinter den Mädchen, die ich meine, wirklich und wahrhaft die Ebene liegt.

IV. Freilich: es ist nicht die Ebene, die ich meine. Nicht die müßigen Moräste zwischen Lucca und Pistoja, über denen die Vögel schnell und ängstlich fliegen, als ob sie fürchteten müde zu werden mitten in dieser haltlosen Traurigkeit. Es sind nicht die faltigen Flächen der Mark, in denen wachsame Flügelmühlen auf den nächsten Wind warten. Und auch die Felder in Westpreußen sind das nicht, die schon fast Meer bedeuten und einen leisen breiten Wellenschlag haben, in dem sie das Gold ihrer Abende langsam sammeln. Es sind einfach die böhmischen Gebreite, reich und ruhig. Und man hebt sich nicht ab von ihnen, man wird nicht ein Einsamer. Immer sind ein paar Kirsch- oder Apfelbäume da, neben denen man unbedeutend und gesellig aussieht, man mag noch so allein und ratlos sein im Herzen.

V. Und, weiß Gott weshalb, ich denke, daß meine Mädchen also sind. Je mehr ihrer beisammen stehen, desto einsamer wird eine jede. Die welche hinzutritt zu dem schweigsamen Schwesterkreis, geht eigentlich fort und das Furchtbare ist, daß keiner weiß wohin. – Ein alter Mann hat mir einmal am Abend gesagt, daß alle Wege, die man nicht kennt, zu Gott führen. Er hat es bestimmt gewußt und ich glaube es ihm auch heute noch. Aber ich fürchte nur, daß meine Mädchen zu ganz verschiedenen Zeiten bei Gott ankommen, so daß die Ersten schon wieder weiter sind, wenn die Zögernden atemlos und mit heißen Gesichtern vor Ihm staunen. Auf diese Weise können sie sich nie und nirgends Alle wiedersehen. Wenn man nämlich annimmt, daß Nichts bei Gott bleibt, sondern über Ihn hinaus strebt, ja

the little smart alecks smile their superior smiles at such realizations. But their smiles about the ocean I've unexpectedly made in the middle of Bohemia are not nearly as bright as the joy with which they imperiously tell themselves, faced with bare floorboards or furrowed fields: that is the ocean. So I'd rather leave creation to them, these little Almighties, and content myself with the fact that behind the girls I'm thinking of there really and truly is a plain.

IV. Of course it's not the plains that I'm thinking of. Not the worthless wastelands between Lucca and Pistoia that the birds fly over quickly and nervously, as though afraid they might run out of energy in the middle of this trackless sadness. It's not the creased surface of the borderlands where vigilant windmills await the next wind. And it's not the fields of West Prussia either, already almost an ocean in themselves, with a soft broad tide of their own where they slowly gather in the gold of their evenings. I'm thinking merely of the expanse of Bohemia, rich and restful. And you don't stand out against it, you aren't isolated. There are always a few cherry or apple trees, next to which you look ordinary and sociable, however alone and helpless you might be in your heart.

V. And, God knows why, that is how I think these girls of mine are. The more they stand together the more solitary each one becomes. The one who joins the silent circle of sisters in fact goes forth alone, and the frightening thing is, no one knows where to. – An old man said to me, one evening, that every unknown path leads to God. He knew it for certain and to this day I believe him. But I'm afraid that my girls all come to God at different times, so that the first ones have already moved on by the time the hesitant ones, breathless and hot in the face, stand stunned before Him. As a result they can never all meet again, never and nowhere. But that's if you assume that nothing stays with God, that everything pushes past Him, in fact maybe only really begins to move once it's found Him.

vielleicht erst recht anfängt sich zu rühren, wenn es Ihn gefunden hat.

VI. Meine Mädchen finden weder, noch suchen sie. Sie können sich überhaupt nicht erinnern, daß sie einmal gesucht haben. Sie wissen nur dunkel von verschiedenen Funden, die in die Zeit vor dem Groß-Werden gehören. Was sich ihnen damals wider Erwarten in die scheuen, braunen Händchen schmiegte oder in die viel scheueren Herzen, das haben sie aufbewahrt all die Jahre lang; mochte es eine verbogene Brosche oder ein verlorenes Wort gewesen sein. Man sinnt so gern, wem die Dinge gedient haben und wozu. Ich habe mich immer, sooft ich einen Fund getan habe, wie ein Erbe gefühlt, der die Herrschaft antritt nach einem unbekannten König. Und aus dieser Erfahrung heraus behaupte ich, daß meine Mädchen die rechtmäßigen Erbinnen vergangener Frauen sind, die schöne und schwere Kronen getragen haben.

VII. Bei Knaben heißt Groß-Werden, mündig werden. Die großen Mädchen aber sind viel unmündiger als die kleinen. Die kleinen küßt man offen und oft; die großen möchte man heimlich küssen. Das ist ein Unterschied und sicher der seltsamsten einer. Die Knaben wachsen so stramm und stetig in ihr Mannsein hinein; auf einmal paßt es ihnen: du weißt nicht wie. Die Mädchen lassen plötzlich ihr Kinderkleid los und stehen furchtsam und frierend da am Anfange eines ganz anderen Lebens, in dem die Worte und die Münzen, welche sie gewohnt waren, nichts mehr gelten. Sie entwickeln sich nur bis an die Schwelle ihrer Reife regelmäßig und ruhig. Von da an verwirren sich die Uhren. Mancher Tag ist wie gar keiner und hinter ihm kommt eine Nacht, die ist: wie tausend Tage.

VIII. Alte Leute vom Land erzählen davon, daß die jungen Mädchen in der guten Zeit, die sie die ihre heißen, an den langen Nachmittagen des Herbstes zu Rocken gingen. In der großen gastlichen Stube, drin sich die ganze Freundschaft sittsam zusammenfand, saßen sie sinnend im Rund, und oft sprach das frühe Feuer für sie, das sich im dachigen Kachelkamin auf dem herrschaftlichen

VI. These girls of mine do not find, nor do they seek. They cannot remember ever once having sought. They know only darkly about various discoveries that belong to the time before they grew up. Whatever surprised them back then and nestled into their shy little brown hands, or into their much shyer hearts, they stored up, all these years, be it a curved brooch or a lost word. People love to brood about things: whom the things served, and why. Whenever I made such a discovery, I always felt like an heir coming to power after an unknown king. And out of this experience comes my conviction that these girls are the rightful heiresses of the bygone women who wore beautiful, heavy crowns.

VII. With boys, growing up means coming of age. Big girls, though, are much less "of age" than little ones. You kiss the little ones often and openly; you want to kiss the big ones in secret. That is a difference, and surely one of the strangest. The boys grow up into their manhood so sturdily and steadily; all of a sudden it fits them, you don't know how. The girls let go of their children's dresses suddenly and stand there, timid and freezing, at the start of a wholly different life, where the words and the coins they are used to are no longer valid currency. They develop regularly and calmly only up to the threshold of their maturity. Then the clocks go haywire. Sometimes a day is like nothing at all and then right on its heels comes a night that is like . . . a thousand days.

VIII. Old people from the country talk about how, in the good old days that they call theirs, young girls went to their distaffs in the long afternoons of autumn. In the big hospitable living room where all their friends would gather together, on their very best behavior, they sat contemplatively in a circle and the early fire, cozily stretched out on the imposing wood in

Holz behaglich ausstreckte. Ein Duft von weißem, feinem Linnen, hausbackenem Rosinenkuchen (nach geheimem Rezept) und heißem prasselndem Tannenharz, richtig gemischt und um meine gütige alte Tante Zdeni sorglich ausgebreitet, könnte wohl bewirken, daß der feinen, greisen Frau manches wieder einfiele, was sie fünfundvierzig Jahre vorher in dieser ahnungsvollen Atmosphäre empfand. Aber wir haben nicht die Mittel diesen wundersamen Weihrauch zu wecken, und meine gütige Tante Zdeni versichert, es müsse sich alles Schöne, was sie damals sann, fest in den Fäden der weißen Gewebe finden, die sie das ganze Jahr unberührt in dem Schranke aus mattem Mahagoni verwahrt hält; denn da es nicht in ihrem langen Leben war, wird es wohl in den Tischtüchern geblieben sein, meint sie.

IX. So ist es immer. Eher webt man seine Träume tief in Tücher ein, als daß man sie so neben dem Leben her wachsen ließe, in dem sie nicht genug Sonne hätten, um auszureifen. Wenn man zu Ende ist, läßt man sie in kleinen und scheinbar wertlosen, altmodischen Dingen zurück, die bis an ihr eigenes Zugrundegehen nichts verraten. Nicht etwa weil sie schweigen, sondern weil sie sentimentale Lieder singen in einer Sprache deren letzter Versteher gestorben ist und für welche es keine Wörterbücher und keine Lehrer giebt. So hilft mir denn auch meiner tugendsamen Ahnin, der Josepha Christin von Goldberg elfenbeinbesetztes Spinnrad nur schlecht zum Verständnis der rockenreifen Mädchen in den kleinen und ganz kleinen Städten meiner Heimat.

X. Sie müssen mir selber helfen. Wundersam ist die Hilfe der Hilflosen und heilig. Ihr Verstummen oder Staunen ist vielleicht ein stärkeres Beistehen als die riesigen Reden, die in der Überzeugung von neunundneunzig Gerechten gedeihen. Und dann: wenn du neunundneunzig Gerechte erst gefunden hast, verzichtest du sicher gerne darauf, sie auch noch reden zu hören; denn es wären dann vielleicht gar nicht mehr neunundneunzig. Meiner Mädchen indessen sind mühelos mehr. Denn wenngleich ich nur die in meiner Heimat zähle, weiß ich doch, daß aus allen Orten, in denen ich ein Ave läuten gehört habe, Viele leise

the covered tiled fireplace, often did their talking for them. A smell of fine white linen, homemade raisin cookies (from a secret recipe), and hot crackling pine resin, all mixed together, solicitously diffused around my kind-hearted old Aunt Zdeni, would probably be able to bring back to this wonderful ancient woman's mind some of what she felt forty-five years before in this same suggestive environment. But we have not the means to draw forth this wondrous scent from its censer, and my kind-hearted Aunt Zdeni assures me that everything beautiful she brooded about back then must be safe in the threads of the white fabric she keeps stored all year long, untouched, in the dull mahogany wardrobe; since it was not to be found in her own long life, it must have stayed in the tablecloths, she says.

IX. That's how it always is. People would sooner weave their dreams deep into the linens than let them grow up next to them into a life without enough sun for them to ripen. When you near your end, you leave your dreams behind in small and seemingly worthless, old-fashioned things, which betray no secrets before they perish in turn. And not because they keep quiet, but because they sing their sentimental songs in a language which no one left alive can understand, for which there is no dictionary and no teacher. So even the ivory-inlaid spinning wheel of my virtuous ancestor, Josepha Christin von Goldberg, does a poor job of helping me understand the girls matured at the distaff in the small towns and tiny villages of my homeland.

X. They have to help me themselves. Wondrous is the help of the helpless, and holy. Their falling silent, their astonishment, may be stronger allies than the mighty speeches that prosper in the strong opinions of the ninety-nine righteous men. And besides: when you have finally found the ninety-nine righteous men, you would surely much rather do without hearing them talk too: who knows if there would still be ninety-nine of them then. My girls, though, are more numerous without even trying. Even if I only count the ones in my homeland, I know that everywhere I heard the bells ring Ave Maria many other girls accompanied

mitgehen, und ich tue als ob ich es nicht bemerkt hätte. So wächst die Wanderzahl langsam an, und ich habe Mühe die Menge zu überschauen, die sich dunkel an mir vorüberdrängt.

XI. Sie sind Schwestern von Gewand. Sie sind Verwandte in ihrer Angst, Abschiednehmende in ihrer Freude und Fremde von Herz zu Herz. Sie haben das Gemeinsame *um* sich und *in* sich je eine eigentümliche Einsamkeit, in der Gebräuche und Gebete gelten, von denen wir uns nicht träumen lassen. Sie sind jede wie eine Religion, die vom Munde eines offenbarenden Gottes unterwegs ist: die zu einem verschmachteten Geschlecht, zu einem schwachgeschwelgten Stamme jene. Sie tragen jede eine Schale voll Erfüllung in den rhythmisch zitternden Händen, aber keine weiß, an welche Lippen ihr glänzendes Gefäß grenzen wird.

XII. In den Büchern stehen die Geschicke derjenigen aufgezeichnet, die besonders glücklich oder unglücklich, besonders heilig oder besonders häßlich von Herzen waren. Dann Episoden aus dem Leben einer jeden; Hoffnungen und Heimlichkeiten, Ohnmachten und Offenbarungen geordnet nach dem Alphabet des Alters und der Erfahrung. Man spricht dort entweder von den Mädchen auf dem Land, oder von den Mädchen in den Städten, oder wohl gar von einem einzigen Mädchen, welches aus dem einen Rahmen in den anderen geschoben wird. Man beschreibt dort entweder ein Mädchen dem nichts oder ein solches dem Alles geschieht; oder mit besonderer Vorliebe wählt man auch da ein Beispiel, an dem sich beides der Reihe nach zeigen läßt, welches als sehr lehrreich und spannend empfunden wird. Das ist nun einmal so Sitte geworden in den Romanen und bei denen, welche sich mit dem Erdichten von Geschichten, Begebenheiten und Schicksalen befassen.

XIII. Man kann nichts gegen diese ruhige und beschauliche Beschäftigung vorbringen; denn die Geschichte des Zoroaster, des Plato, Jesu-Christi, des Columbus, des Lionardo und des Napoléon und noch mehrerer Menschen mußte geschrieben werden, das heißt sie schrieb sich sozusagen von selbst. Eine jede

them in silence. I act as though I haven't noticed. And so the number of wanderers slowly increases, and I have a difficult time commanding a view of the crowd that darkly presses past me.

XI. They are sisters of the vestment. They are related in their fear, bidding farewell from joy, strangers to each other's hearts. What they have in common is *around* them; *in* them they each have their own particular solitude, where practices and prayers apply that we cannot dream of. They are, each one of them, like a religion making its way from the mouth of a self-revealing God: this one making its way to a languishing race, that one to a spoiled, weak line. They carry, each one of them, a dish full of fulfillment in her rhythmically quivering hands, but no one knows whose lips her sparkling vessel will edge.

XII. In books there are recorded the fortunes of those who were especially happy or unhappy, especially holy or hateful in their hearts. Then there are episodes from the life of each one: hopes and revelations, secrets and swoonings, ordered according to the alphabet of age and experience. They talk in those books either about girls in the country or girls in the city, or maybe about an only daughter taken out of one setting and placed into the other. They describe either a girl nothing happens to or a girl everything happens to, but they have a special predilection for cases where both take place, one after the other – this is felt to be particularly thrilling and educational and is now customary in novels and with anyone who deals with manufactured stories, events, and destinies.

XIII. You cannot hold anything against this calm and tranquil occupation: the story of Zoroaster, of Plato, of Jesus Christ and Columbus and Leonardo and Napoleon and many more did need to get written. In other words, these stories wrote themselves, so to speak. Every one of this cast of characters etched a

dieser handelnden Personen zog eine Furche in das große graue Gehirn der Erde, und wir alle tragen eine kleine Reproduktion dieses Urhirnes in uns, nach der Art der Taschenuhren oder der kleinen runden Kompaßpillen, die anzeigen, wo die Sonne aufgeht über einen biederen Bürgerbauch. Später entstand auch die Geschichte seltener Frauen; doch da war schon ein leises Beihelfen notwendig und für das geozentrische Haupthirn war eine Logik und eine Mnemotechnik erfunden worden, auf welche selbst die Historiker von heute stolz sind. In den jüngsten, halbverhallten Jahrhunderten hat man sich immer mehr um das ›paysage intime‹ bemüht, will sagen, man hat die Geschichte der namenlosen Menschen erzählen wollen. Der Eine oder der Andere glaubte nämlich bemerkt zu haben, daß eine Schlacht nicht notwendig bei Thermopylä, Hastings oder Austerlitz, sondern gelegentlich bei Angst, Sehnsucht oder Undank Raum hat, und daß nicht jede Entdeckung auf ein Amerika, nicht jedes Erfinden auf Pulver, Dampfmaschine oder Luftschiff fallen muß, um bedeutend und in einem bestimmten Begriff fruchtbar zu sein. Dabei ist es üblich geworden, statt beglaubigter Helden, glaubhafte hinzustellen. In dieser Absicht zerreißt man seit vielen Jahrzehnten die Heroen der Vergangenheit und die brauchbaren Zeitgenossen und fügt aus unkenntlichen Stücken neue und immer neue Möglichkeiten zusammen, die sich wie interessante oder seltsame Menschen ausnehmen sollen, wenigstens wenn man sie im richtigen Licht und von einer bestimmten Stelle aus betrachtet. Man stellt unablässig Versuche an, erfindet Gesetzmäßigkeiten, vor denen ältere Gesetze mäßig erscheinen, und man hat große Freude, wenn man ein Präparat, dem man den Kopf statt auf dem Rumpf, auf der Zehe des rechten Fußes angeheftet hat, eine Weile lebendig erhält. Dabei wird man klug. Das heißt man legt sich eine Sammlung mehr oder minder ernster Erfahrungen an und muß immer noch ein Zimmer zumieten, um alle Früchte des rüstigen Forscherfleißes unter Dach zu halten. Bei einer solchen Sichtung werten natürlich die seltenen Arten und unerwarteten Nüancen am schwersten. Und es mag sein, daß reife Menschen, die sich heftig von ihrer Umgebung abheben, merkwürdige Dinge erleben und das

furrow in the great gray brain of the earth, and we all carry a miniature reproduction of this archetypal brain within us, like a pocket watch or the small round pill of a compass that shows where the sun rises over a worthy citizen's belly. Later the stories of rare women came into existence; but here a little assistance was necessary, and a logic and a mnemotechnic were invented for the geocentric primary brain that even the historians of today are still proud of. In our most recent century, which has almost died away now, people worked more and more on the *paysage intime* – they wanted to tell the story of the nameless individuals. Someone finally seemed to notice that battles don't only take place at Thermopylae or Hastings or Austerlitz, sometimes the battlefield is called Fear or Desire or Ingratitude; that not every discovery is of America; that not every invention has to arrive at gunpowder or the steam engine or the airship in order to be meaningful and, in a certain sense, fruitful. And so it has become the norm to present not true, authenticated heroes, but plausible, authentic-seeming heroes. To this end they have spent the last few decades ripping apart the heroes of the past and the usable contemporaries and putting together new, ever new possibilities from the unrecognizable pieces. These possibilities are supposed to come across as interesting or singular human beings, at least when you look at them in the right light, from a certain angle. And people keep making these attempts, incessantly, keep manufacturing modern legitimacies that make the old measures seem moderate; they're very happy when one of these specimens, after they attach its head not to its torso but to its right toe, clings to life for a while. That's how people become clever. In other words, they lay in a collection of more or less serious experiences and then have to rent an extra room to hold all the fruits of their vigorous, diligent research. When you look at it this way, of course, the rare types and unexpected nuances count most heavily. And it may indeed be that mature human beings, standing in sharp contrast to their surroundings, do experience strange things, and in the strangest way too. It is said that their "fate" is of the greatest interest, and two things are meant by this word:

obendrein auf die merkwürdigste Art. Man pflegt zu sagen: ihr
›Schicksal‹ begründe das größere Interesse, und man meint
damit zweierlei: das, was ihnen von außen zustößt, und ihr Ver-
hältnis und Verhalten den Angriffen und Eindrücken gegenüber.

XIV. Wenn ich aus meinen vielen Mädchen und einigen Bruch-
stücken Jeanne d'Arc, Charlotte Corday und Katharina Emmerich
/ um nur *eine* Mischungsmöglichkeit zu streifen / *eine* Gestalt
zusammenfüge, dann kann auch ich mich einer Heldin rüh-
men, die, wenn sie sich erst ans Bücken gewöhnt hat, in den
Häusern der kleinen Städte gern und gastlich verkehren wird.
Aber meine Mädchen seh ich bange werden. Sie fürchten, ich
würde sie über alle Abgründe zu einander zerren, und von der
Einen das und von der Zweiten ein Anderes und von keiner
alles wollen; sie haben Angst, daß sie als Halbverschmähte mit
der halben Habe in den enttäuschten Händen zurückbleiben,
wie weiße Rosen durch die ein Sturm gegangen ist mit breiten,
rücksichtslosen, schrecklichen Schultern.

XV. Da sehe ich in ihren Gesichtern und Gestalten hundert
und hundert Bangigkeiten. Klare und dunkle, traumhafte und
wachsame, entsagende und sehnsüchtige Ängste drängen auf
mich zu oder fliehen furchtsam vor meinem Blick ins Unbe-
stimmte. Da weiß ich, daß ich nicht zehn oder zwanzig Mädchen
zu einer Heldin zusammenzwingen darf. Ich muß vielmehr die
Eine, an die ich denke, ausbreiten über alle tausend Schwestern,
die sie immer begleiten. Nur wenn ich von tausend Mädchen
rede, wird es scheinen, daß ich von einem etwas Liebes und
Heimliches weiß; nur wenn unzählige ihre Stimmen vereinen,
wird auch der Fernste und der Traurigste einen Hauch jenes
hohen Liedes spüren, das seinesgleichen nicht hat.

XVI. Fra Fiesole hat in den großen Freskobildern, auf denen er
einsame strenge Gestalten darstellt, in jeder die Hoffnung auf
den Himmel schlicht und schön ausgesprochen. Aber auf
den vielen, vielen gottatmenden Angesichten der Engel des
›Jüngsten Gerichtes‹ hat der Himmel selber mit Heiterkeit und

that which strikes them from without, and their actions and reactions when faced with these blows and impressions.

XIV. If I were to put together *one* figure from my many girls and from fragments of Joan of Arc, Charlotte Corday, and Anna Katharina Emmerich – just to touch on *one* possible combination – then I too could sing the praises of a heroine who would be happily and hospitably welcomed into the houses of the small towns if she were willing to stoop so low. But I see my girls getting scared. They are afraid I will haul them across all the abysses to each other, and will want this from one and that from another and *everything* from none of them; they are scared of being left behind as half-requited lovers with half of what they possess in their disappointed hands, like white roses a storm has moved through with its broad, merciless, terrifying shoulders.

XV. And then I see, in their faces and figures, hundreds and hundreds of apprehensions. Clear and dark, dreaming and waking, renouncing and desiring fears press in on me or flee in fright from my glance to someplace undefined. Then I know that I mustn't cram ten or twenty girls together into one heroine. Instead I need to take one, think about her, and spread her out across the thousand sisters who are always with her. Only when I speak of a thousand girls will I seem to know something private and tender about one; only when their countless voices unite will even the saddest one and the one farthest away feel a breath of that high song which has no equal.

XVI. Fra Angelico, in his great frescoes of severe solitary figures, expressed the aspiration to Heaven simply and beautifully in every one. But on the many, many God-breathing faces of the angels in the *Last Judgment*, Heaven itself has its place with all its serenity and sovereignty and song. These faces are the many-

Hoheit und Hymnen Raum. Sie sind das farbenfältige Mosaik seiner Macht, und es giebt seiner kein Bild, welches gleich groß und reich und ergreifend wäre.

XVII. Frauen hat es viele gegeben. Müde, wie die blonde Maria, böse wie Berechta von Rosenberg, welche vor dem Tode her leise durch Böhmens Burgen geht, und gute wie Elisabeth, die liebliche Landgräfin von Thüringen, deren Bangnis Rosen aus Brot blühen heißt. Und dann die vielen Mütter überhaupt. Aber hat es schon Mädchen gegeben vor meinen Mädchen? Auf keinem Wege kannst du die Spur solcher Füße finden. Umsonst suchst du diesen leichten Abdruck in allem Sand. Er ist wie ein Mal auf der Wange eines Kindes, das auf seinem Händchen geschlafen hat. Winzige Mulden bleiben im Weg, wie unter der Last einer Liebkosung zurück – hinter den Mädchen; *vor* ihnen ist Alles glatt und blank. Entweder sind sie also die ersten, oder die vor ihnen sind immer über Wiesen gegangen oder über dunkles, duftendes Moos oder über das Meer?

XVIII. Wird jemand wissen: daß auch auf dem Steinpflaster des Bürgersteiges kein Bild des Fußes bleibt. Darauf ist zu antworten: daß es in diesen kleinen Städten noch nicht allzuviel eingemauerte Gassen giebt. Wenigstens der Fahrdamm ist fast überall noch ein Strom Staubes, aus dem man sich nach den festeren Rändern retten mag. Aber meine Mädchen schreiten mitten durch; immer dort, wo sie viel Himmel über sich fühlen, und auf kleinen weißen Wolken gehn sie durch die ganze Stadt. Mit keinem Woher hinter sich und so ohne Wohin. Gehen einfach. Vielleicht, damit sie ihr Blut nicht so laut branden hören. Gehen im tastenden Takte dieses heimlichen Wellenschlages. Sind der stille Strand ihrer ruhlosen Unendlichkeit. Finden niemals den gleichen Schritt. Wanken gegen einander, wie von vielen, feindlichen Winden bewegt. Winken jede anderswohin. Wenden zögernd an der Ecke um, wenn der Wind ihnen Worte von den Lippen reißt, die sie noch nicht gewollt haben. Den gleichen Weg kommen sie zurück, und immer wieder wandern sie hin und her zwischen zwei Gassen. Wie Wartende sind sie.

colored mosaic of Heaven's power, and there is no other picture of Heaven which could be as great and rich and gripping.

XVII.   There have been many women. Tired like blonde Maria, bad like Perchta von Rosenberg who softly paces through the castles of Bohemia with death behind her, good like Elisabeth of Hungary, the lovely landgravine of Thuringia, whose trepidation called forth roses from her bread. And then the many mothers. But were there girls before my girls? You cannot find the traces of feet like theirs on any path. In vain would you seek the faintest footprint in all the sand in the world. It is like the mark on the cheek of a child who has slept on his little hand. Tiny hollows are left on the path, like those left under the weight of a caress – behind the girls; *in front* of them all is smooth and empty. So maybe they are the first, or did those before them always walk across the fields, or across dark, fragrant mosses, or on water across the sea?

XVIII.   Someone insists: There are no footprints to be found on a sidewalk's pavement either. To that I reply: There are not many paved sidewalks in these small towns yet. Certainly the street itself, where the vehicles go, is almost everywhere still a river of dust, from which you escape to the firmer roadsides. But my girls stride straight down the middle of the street, wherever they can feel the most sky above them, and they walk through the whole town on little white clouds. With no whence behind them, so without any whither. Just walking. Maybe so that they won't hear the tides of their blood surge so loud. Walking in the tentative rhythm of this secret inner beat of the surf. They are the silent shore of their restless infinity. They never find the same pace. They bump into each other as though blown by a host of inimical winds. Wave in different directions. Turn the corner, hesitating, when the wind tears words from their lips which they didn't yet intend. Come back the same way, and wander back and forth again and again between two streets. Like someone waiting. Always finish their roaming around

Irren immer in einer einzigen Viertelstunde herum. Statt hinauszuziehen in die Zeit wie eine weiße Prozession mit einer fremden feurigen Fahne.

XIX. Geh hinter ihnen einmal. Unwillkürlich senkt sich dein Blick; denn ihre lichten Kleider blenden. Dein Auge fällt mit halbversengten Flügeln auf den Fahrdamm, der wie ein breites Buch und aufgeschlagen ist. In seine Blätter haben vergangene Wagen Linien gelegt. Und das ist gut. Denn die Schritte der Mädchen können nicht grade schreiben. Viele Schriften führen die Furchen entlang. Auf und ab. Als ob jemand bei Nacht geschrieben hätte oder wie Briefe von Blinden. Und doch merkt man bei einiger Mühe und Übung, daß das lauter lange Gedichte sind, Improvisationen, durch die wachsend und wechselnd ein seltsamer Rhythmus rinnt. Die gleichen Reimworte kehren immer wieder. Wie Flehende. Du findest dieselben an allen Türen warten. Rührende, schlichte Worte sind es, Lauten, welche nur eine einzige Saite haben. Eine silberne, – denkst du; und du lässest dich von ihrem Ton begleiten bis in den Traum.

XX. Wenn meine Mädchen wandern und sich bewegen, schwanken ihre Seelen langsam wie Kähne, die an ein unruhiges Ufer gebunden sind. – Denn ihre Seelen sind Gondeln von Gold und voller Ungeduld. Sie sind ganz verhangen mit alten, sanften seidenen Stoffen, so daß es ewig dämmert in ihnen. Die Mädchen lieben dieses duftende Dunkel mit seinen schönen unerschöpften Möglichkeiten. Sie wohnen darin. Selten, wenn die Falten des Vorhangs sich rühren, ritzt sie das Licht. Und sie staunen dann einen Augenblick ein Stück Stube an oder einen Garten, der gerade Abend hat. Und sie erschrecken leise, daß es Stube und Garten und Abend giebt. Und sie heben die Furcht vor diesen vielen Dingen in das seidene Dunkel ihres Lebens hinein und falten die Hände davor. So sind ihre Gebete . . .

XXI. . . . .
. . . .
. . . .

within fifteen minutes. Instead of venturing out into time like a white procession with a fiery foreign flag.

XIX. Go walk behind them. Your gaze will involuntarily lower; their bright clothes are blinding. Your eye will fall with wings half singed off onto the road, which lies spread out and wide like an open book. In its pages, bygone carriages have laid down their lines. And that is good. For the steps of the girls can't write straight. Many lines of writings run alongside the furrows. Up and down. As if someone had written them at night, or like the letters of the blind. Still, with a little effort and practice, you can tell that these are nothing less than long poems, improvisations, through which, waxing and waning, runs a strange rhythm. The same rhyme-words return again and again. As if pleading. You find the same ones waiting at every door. They are moving, simple words; lutes with only a single string. A silver string, you think – and its note can bring you all the way into a dream.

XX. When these girls of mine wander and roam, their souls slowly sway like rowboats tied to an unsteady shore. – For their souls are gondolas of gold, laden with impatience. They are completely draped with old, soft, silken fabrics, so that dusk is eternally falling within them. The girls love this sweet-smelling darkness with its lovely inexhausted possibilities. They live in it. On rare occasions, when the folds of the curtain stir, the light scratches them. And then for a moment they stare, astonished, at a corner of the room or a garden where it is just evening. They are quietly terrified that room and garden and evening exist, and they lift the fear of these many things into the silken darkness of their lives and fold their hands over it. Thus are their prayers.

XXI. . . . .
. . . .
. . . .

Ein junges Mädchen: das ist wie ein Stern:
die ganze Erde dunkelt ihm entgegen
und ist ihm aufgetan wie einem Regen,
und niemals trank sie einen seligern.

Ein junges Mädchen: das ist wie ein Schatz,
vergraben neben einer alten Linde;
da sollen Ringe sein und Goldgewinde,
doch keiner ist erwählt, daß er sie finde:
nur eine Sage geht und sagt den Platz.

Ein junges Mädchen: daß wir's niemals sind.
So wenig hat das Sein zu uns Vertrauen.
Am Anfang scheinen wir fast gleich, als Kind,
und später sind wir manchmal beinah Frauen
für einen Augenblick; doch wie verrinnt
das fern von uns, was Mädchen sind und schauen.

Mädchen gewesen sein: daß es das giebt.
Als sagte Eine: einmal war ich dies
und zeigte dir ein Halsband von Türkis
auf welkem Sammte; und man sieht noch, wie's
getragen war, verloren und geliebt.

Young Girl

background vs. foreground (45.)

A young girl: she is like a star:
the whole world's darker when she's there;
it opens to her as to the rain
and never drank a holier.

A young girl: she is like a treasure:
buried by an old linden tree;
a cache of rings and golden garlands,
but no one is chosen, none can find her,
there's only a legend to tell us where.

A young girl: we will never be one.
Being has so little faith in us.
At first, as children, we seemed almost
the same, and later nearly women,
for a moment; but it passes so far
away from us – what girls see, and are.

To have been a girl: at least there's that.
As though someone said: once I was this,
and showed you a neckband made of turquoise
on faded velvet, and you could still see
how it was worn, and lost, and loved.

La Dame à la Licorne
(*Teppiche im Hôtel de Cluny*)

für Stina Frisell
Zum Gedächtnis gemeinsamen Schauens und Erlebens
vor den Teppichen der edlen Dame aus dem Hause
Le Viste im Hôtel de Cluny. 9. Juni 1906. Paris.

Frau und Erlauchte: sicher kränken wir
oft Frauen-Schicksal das wir nicht begreifen.
Wir sind für euch die Immer-noch-nicht-Reifen
für euer Leben, das, wenn wir es streifen
ein Einhorn wird, ein scheues, weißes Tier,

das flüchtet ... und sein Bangen ist so groß,
daß ihr es selber / wie es schlank entschwindet /
nach vielem Traurigsein erst wiederfindet,
noch immer schreckhaft, warm und atemlos.

Dann bleibt ihr bei ihm, fern von uns, – und mild
gehn durch des Tagwerks Tasten eure Hände;
demütig dienen euch die Gegenstände,
ihr aber wollt nur *diesen* Wunsch gestillt:
daß einst das Einhorn sein beruhigtes Bild
in eurer Seele schwerem Spiegel fände. –

The Lady and the Unicorn
(*Tapestries in the Hôtel de Cluny*)

for Stina Frisell,
In memory of viewing and experiencing together the
tapestries of the noble lady from the house of Le Viste,
at the Cluny in Paris. June 9, 1906.

Lady, Your Ladyship – : how we must wound
that woman-fate we do not understand.
We men are never quite ready for you, quite
ripe for your life; when we brush against it
it turns into a unicorn – shy and white

and running away. . . . So scared that only
after many sorrows can you find it again,
– oh how it slips away – even then
it is skittish, and warm, and out of breath.

Then you stay with it, far from us – your hands   *Tagwerks*
move softly through the touch of your daily tasks;
objects serve you humbly, with respect;
but you want only *one* longing met:
that one day the unicorn find its image, calm,
in the heavy mirror of your souls. –

heavy mirror of your souls.

Vielleicht war es immer so. Vielleicht war immer eine weite
Fremde zwischen einer Zeit und der großen Kunst, welche in ihr
entstand. Vielleicht waren die Kunstwerke immer so einsam,
wie sie es heute sind, und vielleicht war der Ruhm niemals
etwas anderes als der Inbegriff aller Mißverständnisse, die sich
um einen neuen Namen versammeln. Es liegt kein Grund vor zu
glauben, daß es jemals anders war. Denn das, was die Kunstwerke
unterscheidet von allen anderen Dingen, ist der Umstand, daß
sie gleichsam zukünftige Dinge sind, Dinge, deren Zeit noch
nicht gekommen ist. Die Zukunft, aus der sie stammen, ist fern;
sie sind die Dinge jenes letzten Jahrhunderts, mit welchem ein-
mal der große Kreis der Wege und Entwicklungen sich schließt,
sie sind die vollkommenen Dinge und Zeitgenossen des Gottes,
an dem die Menschen seit Anbeginn bauen und den sie noch
lange nicht vollenden werden. Wenn es trotzdem scheint, als
ob die großen Kunstdinge vergangener Epochen mitten im
Rauschen ihrer Zeiten gestanden hätten, so mag man dies damit
erklären, daß den entfernten Tagen (von denen wir so wenig
wissen) jene letzte und wunderbare Zukunft, welche die Heimat
der Kunstwerke ist, näher war als uns. Das Morgen schon war
ein Teil des Weiten und Unbekannten, es lag hinter jedem Grab,
und die Götterbilder waren die Grenzsteine eines Reichs tiefer
Erfüllungen. Langsam entfernte sich diese Zukunft von den
Menschen. Glaube und Aberglaube drängte sie hinaus in immer
größere Fernen, Liebe und Zweifel warf sie über die Sterne
hinaus und in die Himmel hinein. Unsere Lampen endlich
sind weitsichtig geworden, unsere Instrumente reichen über
Morgen und Übermorgen, wir entziehen mit den Mitteln der
Forschung kommende Jahrhunderte der Zukunft und machen
sie zu einer Art noch nicht begonnener Gegenwart. Die
Wissenschaft hat sich aufgerollt wie ein weiter, unabsehbarer
Weg, die schweren und schmerzhaften Entwicklungen der

On Completing the Circle

I Works of Art (*January 1903, age twenty-seven*)

Maybe it was always that way. Maybe there was always a vast and strange alienation between an era and the great art which arises in it. Maybe works of art were always as solitary as they are today, and maybe fame was never anything but the distillation of all the misunderstandings that gather around a new name. There is no reason to believe that it was ever any different. For what distinguishes works of art from everything else is the fact that they are, as it were, of the future: things whose time has not yet come. The future they come from is far away; they belong to that final century with which the great circle of paths and developments will be completed; they are the perfected things, the contemporaries of the God that people have been constructing since the beginning and have not come anywhere near completing. If it nevertheless seems as though the great art objects of bygone eras stood in the middle of the surging current of their times, the explanation is that this final, wonderful future, the true home of works of art, was closer to remote times (of which we know so little) than it is to us. Back then, even tomorrow's dawn was part of the distant and unknown that lay behind every grave, and images of God were boundary stones marking the edge of a kingdom of deep fulfillments. Slowly, this future distanced itself from us. Belief and superstition drove it away to greater and greater distances, love and doubt hurled it out past the stars into the heavens. And now we have reached a point when our lights let us see far; our instruments reach past tomorrow and the day after that; with our researches we extract the coming centuries out of the future and turn them into a sort of not yet begun present. Science has unrolled itself like a long, unforeseeable path, and difficult, painful developments, of both individuals and the masses, have filled in the coming millenniums with an unending task and duty.

And far, far behind all that lies the home of works of art,

Menschen, der einzelnen und der Massen, füllen die nächsten Jahrtausende als eine unendliche Aufgabe und Arbeit aus.

Und weit, weit hinter alledem, liegt die Heimat der Kunstwerke, jener seltsam verschwiegenen und geduldigen Dinge, die fremd umherstehen unter den Dingen täglichen Gebrauches, unter den beschäftigten Menschen, den dienenden Tieren und den spielenden Kindern.

[...] nach den großen Anstrengungen des vorigen Jahrs...

Einer solchen Arbeitsausgabe folgt jedes Mal ein Ratlossein, nicht daß man eigentlich leer wäre, aber bestimmte Vorräte des eigenen Wesens sind verwandelt, sind fortgegeben und gleichsam dem eigenen persönlichen Gebrauche für immer entzogen. Man mag sich nicht sofort nach anderem inneren Besitz umsehen – man weiß eigentlich nicht, *was* man mag, es ist ein Zustand des Zögerns, des Sich-langsam-Umwendens, – und es zeigt sich, daß man in solcher Zeit ungern »Ich« sagt –, denn was wäre, ohne Anstrengung und Zwang, von solchem Ich auszusagen? Oft in solchen Momenten, früher, kam mir dann ein äußerer Wechsel zustatten, was sowohl dem Ausruhen wie dem Neuanfangen günstig war (– ein Teil meiner Unstetheit mag sich sogar daraus erklären, daß ich jedesmal nach Ablauf einer derartigen Intensitätsperiode *jede* Veränderung, die sich von außen anbot, als eine erwünschte Hülfe hinnahm...); auch diesmal wäre es vielleicht so gekommen, ich war entschlossen, Muzot zu verlassen, sei es, um wieder nach Paris zu ziehen (was für gewisse Studien, die ich vorhabe, längst geboten wäre), sei es, um unsere – mir selber noch unbekannte – Urheimat, Kärnten aufzusuchen und zu sehen, ob dort eine Niederlassung möglich wäre... Das Familienwappen, ich glaube mit einer Jahreszahl des vierzehnten Jahrhunderts, soll noch im Ständehaus in Klagenfurt, immer wieder aufgefrischt, vorkommen, – und ich, nicht allein weil ich der letzte Männliche meines Stammes bin, fühlte mich ganz geeignet, einen solchen weiten Kreis durch eine Art Heimkehr dorthin, wenn das ohne Gewaltsamkeit möglich ist, zu schließen, um mich für einige Zeit dort anzusiedeln,

these strangely silent and patient things that stand around in all their otherness among the things we use every day, among all the busy people, the beasts of burden, the playing children.

II (*January 1923, age forty-seven*)

After a great strain, like my production of work last year, there always comes a feeling of being at a loss: not that you are actually empty but certain things you had stockpiled in your being have been transformed, given away, and as it were withdrawn from personal use forever. You don't want to look around for other inner possessions right away – you don't know *what* you want to do, it is a condition of hesitation, of slowly turning to face another direction – and one sign of being in this state is that you don't like to say "I." Because what is there to say about this "I" without strain and constraint? At such moments earlier in my life, I often found that an external change was useful, beneficial for recuperation and equally for a new beginning (– part of what has made my life so unstable, in fact, may be that every time a period of intensity like this had run its course I took *any* change that offered itself from outside as the help I was looking for . . .); it might have turned out that way this time too. I decided to leave Muzot, either to move back to Paris (a move which was long overdue for certain projects I have in mind) or to visit Carinthia, my ancestral homeland – where I myself have never been – and see whether it might be possible to set myself up there. . . . I hear that a family coat of arms, dating from I think the fourteenth century, has been preserved to this day in an estate assembly house in Klagenfurt. And I felt, not only because I am the last male of my line, like the right person to complete a grand circle by a sort of homecoming there, if it would be possible without too much violent activity, the right one to settle for a while in the place from which, legend and tradition assures us, we went forth! –But then the least effort to

von wo wir, wie Legende und Überlieferung versichert, ausge-
gangen sind! – Aber dann war der mindeste Versuch, beweglich
zu werden, sofort mit soviel Schwierigkeiten verbunden, daß
ich, mehr und mehr, nachgab und mich noch für einen Win-
ter auf Muzot einschloß, im besten Entschluß auch die dies-
malige Klausur so fruchtbar als möglich zu machen. Ich nahm
denn auch gleich verschiedene Übersetzungsarbeiten auf, die
mich wohl durch die stillen Monate hin reichlich beschäftigen
werden [. . . .]

Switzerland

detach myself was immediately bound up with so many diffi-
culties that I put it off, more and more, and then cloistered
myself for another winter in Muzot, with the best intentions of
making this year's seclusion as fruitful as possible too. I imme-
diately took on several translation projects, which should keep
me fully busy through the quiet months. . . .

À Mademoiselle Sophy Giauque

C'est notre extrême labeur :
de trouver une écriture
qui résiste aux pleurs
et qui devant nous re-figure,
précis dans leur clarté pure,
les beaux adieux navigateurs.

Dedication

to Mademoiselle Sophy Giauque

Our greatest task is this:
to find a written language
which can withstand our tears
and re-create before us
– clear, pure, precise –
the beautiful goodbyes
of those who sailed the seas.

— transcends us/our solitude

(63)——

41

> finding commonality
through our own solitude___
in order to use that power
that binds humanity together

...written on
June 26, 1926

(died Dec. 29, 1926)

Vitali erwachte

Vitali erwachte. Er konnte sich nicht erinnern, ob er geträumt hatte. Aber er wußte, daß ein Flüstern ihn weckte. Unwillkürlich sah er nach der Uhr. Es war wenig nach vier. Durch die Dämmerung des Zimmers ging ein gleichmäßiges Hellwerden. Er erhob sich und trat in seiner weißen wollenen Schlafkutte, die ihm das Aussehen eines jungen Mönches gab, ans Fenster. Da lag der kleine Garten vor ihm – still und leer. Es mußte nachts geregnet haben. Durch schwarze kahle Äste sah man den dunklen Boden, der schwer und satt schien, als ob die Nacht, flüchtend, in ihn zurückgesunken wäre, statt sich zu den Himmeln zu erheben. Die Höhen waren öde, umwölkt und von hohen Winden bewegt. Aber als Vitali den Blick ziellos über die Wolken zog, hörte er wieder das Flüstern, und jetzt erst wußte er, daß das frühe ferne Lerchen sind, die den Morgen feiern. Ihre Stimmen waren überall, fern und nah, wie aufgelöst in der lauen tauenden Luft, so daß man sie mehr mit dem Gefühl empfing, als mit dem Ohr. Und er begriff mit einem Male, daß diese Stunde voll Stimmen mit keinem Namen zu nennen ist und auf keiner Uhr abzulesen. Daß noch nicht Morgen ist und nicht mehr Nacht. Er näherte sich mit seinem Gefühle dem Garten unter den Fenstern, als ob er sein Gesicht nun besser verstünde; und er erkannte, den er früher nicht bemerkt hatte, den starken Strauch, auf dessen Ästen, groß wie kleine Vögel, Knospen saßen und warteten. Und Alles da unten war Erwartung und Geduld. Die Bäume und die kleinen runden Beete, die man schon vorbereitet hatte auf etwas Neues, erwarteten den Tag von den Himmeln, und zwar keinen sonnigen, strahlenden Tag, einen Tag, aus dem der Regen fiel, ohne sich wehzutun, weil alles in der Natur Hand ward, die ihn empfing. So rührend geduldete sich der kleine Garten. Vitali aber sagte laut über ihn hin: Wie durch ein gotisches Fenster schaue ich. Dann trat er zurück und ging mit ruhigen Schritten zu seinem Lager. Willig nahm er den Schlaf auf sich. Er hörte aber noch, wie draußen ein großer Regen begann und rauschte.

Vitali Awoke

Vitali awoke. He could not remember whether he'd had any dreams. But he knew that a whisper had woken him. Instinctively he looked at the clock: it was a little past four. A regular, uniform brightening came into the room's semi-darkness. He stood up and, in his white wool bedrobe, which gave him the appearance of a young monk, walked over to the window. The little garden lay there before him – silent, empty. It must have rained in the night. Through black bare branches he could see the dark ground; it looked heavy and full, as though night, fleeing, had sunk back down into it instead of rising up into the heavens. The heights were desolate, shrouded in clouds and moving in the high winds. But while Vitali's glance moved aimlessly across the clouds he heard the whisper again, and only now realized it was the distant early skylarks, celebrating the dawn. Their voices were everywhere, near and far, as though dissolved in the lukewarm thawing air, so that you felt them more than hearing them with your ear. And he knew at once that this hour full of voices cannot be named with any name and cannot be read on any clock. That it is not yet morning and no longer night. With this feeling he drew near to the garden beneath his windows, as though he understood its face better now; he saw something he had never noticed before, the strong bush on whose branches the buds, big as small birds, sat and waited. Everything down there was expectation and patience. The trees and the small round flowerbeds, already prepared for something new, awaited day from the heavens, and in truth they expected not a bright sunny day but a day from which rain would fall, without hurting itself because everything in nature had become a hand to receive it. So touching, this little garden's patience. Vitali, though, said out loud across the garden: *It's like looking through a Gothic window*. Then he walked with calm steps back to his bed. Obediently he took sleep upon himself. But he still heard how, outside, a heavy rain started to fall and then rushed down.

I. Ganz am Anfang sind wir, siehst du.
Wie vor Allem. Mit
Tausend und einem Traum hinter uns und
ohne Tat.

II. Ich kann mir kein seligeres Wissen denken,
als dieses Eine:
daß man ein Beginner werden muß.
Einer der das erste Wort schreibt hinter einen
jahrhundertelangen
Gedankenstrich.

III. Das fällt mir ein: bei dieser Beobachtung: daß wir die Menschen noch immer auf Goldgrund malen, wie die ganz Primitiven. Vor etwas Unbestimmtem stehen sie. Manchmal vor Gold, manchmal auch vor Grau. Im Licht manchmal, und oft mit unergründlichem Dunkel hinter sich.

IV. Man begreift das. Um die Menschen zu erkennen, mußte man sie isolieren. Aber nach einer langen Erfahrung ist es billig, die Einzelbetrachtungen wieder in ein Verhältnis zu setzen, und mit gereiftem Blick ihre breiteren Gebärden zu begleiten.

V. Vergleiche einmal ein Goldgrundbild aus dem Trecento mit einer von den zahlreichen späteren Kompositionen italienischer Frühmeister, wo die Gestalten zu einer *Santa Conversazione* vor der leuchtenden Landschaft in der lichten Luft Umbriens sich zusammenfinden. Der Goldgrund isoliert eine jede, die Landschaft glänzt hinter ihnen wie eine gemeinsame Seele, aus der heraus sie ihr Lächeln und ihre Liebe holen.

VI. Dann denke an das Leben selbst. Erinnere dich, daß die Menschen viele und bauschige Gebärden und unglaublich große

Notes on the Melody of Things

I.   We are right at the start, do you see.
As though before everything. With
a thousand and one dreams behind us and
no act.

II.   I can imagine no knowledge holier
than this:
that you must become a beginner.
Someone who writes the first word after a
centuries-long
dash.

III.   That occurs to me: when I observe: that we still always paint people against a gold background, exactly like the medieval Primitives. People stand before something indefinite – sometimes gold, sometimes gray. Sometimes they stand in the light, and often with an unfathomable darkness behind them.

IV.   That makes sense. To know people we have to isolate them. But after experiencing them for a long time it is only right to put these isolated observations back into a relationship with each other, and follow their broader gestures with a more mature gaze.

V.   Compare a painting with a gold background from the trecento to one of the countless later compositions of the Italian old masters, where the figures assemble in a *Santa Conversazione* in front of a radiant landscape in the light air of Umbria. The gold background isolates each figure; the landscape shines behind them like a common soul from which they draw their smiles and their love.

VI.   Then think about life itself. Remember that people have many, puffed-up gestures and unbelievably grand words. If only

Worte haben. Wenn sie nur eine Weile so ruhig und reich wären, wie die schönen Heiligen des Marco Basaiti, müßtest du auch hinter ihnen die Landschaft finden, die ihnen gemeinsam ist.

VII. Und es giebt ja auch Augenblicke, da sich ein Mensch vor dir still und klar abhebt von seiner Herrlichkeit. Das sind seltene Feste, welche du niemals vergißt. Du liebst diesen Menschen fortan. Das heißt du bist bemüht die Umrisse seiner Persönlichkeit, wie du sie in jener Stunde erkannt hast, nachzuzeichnen mit deinen zärtlichen Händen.

VIII. Die Kunst tut dasselbe. Sie ist ja die weitere, unbescheidenere Liebe. Sie ist die Liebe Gottes. Sie darf nicht bei dem Einzelnen stehen bleiben, der nur die Pforte des Lebens ist. Sie muß ihn durchwandern. Sie darf nicht müde werden. Um sich zu erfüllen muß sie dort wirken, wo Alle – *Einer* sind. Wenn sie dann diesen *Einen* beschenkt, kommt grenzenloser Reichtum über Alle.

IX. Wie weit sie davon ist, mag man auf der Bühne sehen, wo sie doch sagt oder sagen will, wie sie das Leben, nicht den Einzelnen in seiner idealen Ruhe, sondern die Bewegung und den Verkehr Mehrerer betrachtet. Dabei ergiebt sich, daß sie die Menschen einfach neben einander stellt, wie die im Trecento es taten, und es ihnen selbst überläßt sich mit einander zu befreunden über das Grau oder das Gold des Hintergrundes hin.

X. Und darum wird es auch so. Mit Worten und Gesten suchen sie sich zu erreichen. Sie renken sich fast die Arme aus, denn die Gebärden sind viel zu kurz. Sie machen unendliche Anstrengungen die Silben einander zuzuwerfen und sind dabei noch herzlich schlechte Ballspieler, die nicht auffangen können. So vergeht die Zeit mit Bücken und Suchen – ganz wie im Leben.

XI. Und die Kunst hat nichts getan, als uns die Verwirrung gezeigt in welcher wir uns meistens befinden. Sie hat uns

they spent a little time being as rich and peaceful as the beautiful saints of Marco Basaiti, then you would be able to find behind them too the landscape they have in common.

VII. There are, in fact, moments when a person stands out from his grandeur in clarity and silence before you. These are rare festive pleasures that you never forget. You love this person from then on. In other words, you work to retrace with your own tender hands the outlines of the personality that you came to know in this hour.

VIII. Art does the same thing. For art is a farther reaching, more immodest love. It is God's love. It cannot stop with an individual, who is only the portal of life itself: it must move through that individual. It cannot tire. To fulfill its destiny, it has to appear where everyone is – a *someone*. Then it bestows its gifts on this *someone*, and boundless riches come over everyone.

IX. How far art really is from this calling we can see in the theater, for theater does say, or try to say, how it sees life itself: not the individual's life in its ideal stillness but the movement and interaction of many individuals. In the process, though, it simply puts people next to each other, as in the trecento, and leaves it up to them to form closer relationships with each other in front of the background of gray or gold.

X. So that becomes how it is. They try to reach each other with words and gestures. They almost tear their arms out of their sockets, because the reach of their gesticulations is much too short. They try as hard as they can to throw syllables at each other, but they are still extraordinarily bad at this game: they cannot catch. And so time passes, while they stoop over and hunt around for the ball – just like in life.

XI. Art has accomplished nothing, except to show us the confusion in which we already find ourselves most of the time.

beängstigt, statt uns still und ruhig zu machen. Sie hat bewiesen, daß wir jeder auf einer anderen Insel leben; nur sind die Inseln nicht weit genug um einsam und unbekümmert zu bleiben. Einer kann den Anderen stören oder schrecken oder mit Speeren verfolgen – nur helfen kann keiner keinem.

XII. Von Eiland zu Eiland giebt es nur eine Möglichkeit: gefährliche Sprünge, bei denen man mehr als die Füße gefährdet. Ein ewiges Hin- und Herhüpfen entsteht mit Zufällen und Lächerlichkeiten; denn es kommt vor, daß zwei zueinander springen, gleichzeitig, so daß sie einander nur in der Luft begegnen, und nach diesem mühsamen Wechsel ebenso weit sind – Eines vom Anderen – wie vorher.

XIII. Das ist weiter nicht wunderlich; denn in der Tat sind die Brücken zu einander, darüber man schön und festlich gegangen kommt, nicht *in* uns, sondern hinter uns, ganz wie auf den Landschaften des Fra Bartholome oder des Lionardo. Es ist doch so, daß das Leben sich zuspitzt in den einzelnen Persönlichkeiten. Von Gipfel zu Gipfel aber geht der Pfad durch die breiteren Tale.

XIV. Wenn zwei oder drei Menschen zusammenkommen, sind sie deshalb noch nicht beisammen. Sie sind wie Marionetten deren Drähte in verschiedenen Händen liegen. Erst wenn *eine* Hand alle lenkt, kommt eine Gemeinsamkeit über sie, welche sie zum Verneigen zwingt oder zum Dreinhauen. Und auch die Kräfte des Menschen sind dort, wo seine Drähte enden in einer haltenden herrschenden Hand.

XV. Erst in der gemeinsamen Stunde, in dem gemeinsamen Sturm, in der einen Stube, darin sie sich begegnen, finden sie sich. Erst bis ein Hintergrund hinter ihnen steht, beginnen sie miteinander zu verkehren. Sie müssen sich ja berufen können auf die *eine* Heimat. Sie müssen einander gleichsam die Beglaubigungen zeigen, welche sie mit sich tragen und

It has frightened us, rather than making us quiet and peaceful. It has shown us that we all live on different islands, only the islands are not far enough apart for us to stay solitary and untroubled. Someone on one island can pester someone on another, or terrorize him, or hunt him with spears – the only thing no one can do to anyone else is help him.

XII. There is only one way to journey from isle to isle: dangerous leaps in which more than one's feet are endangered. The result is an eternal hopping back and forth, with accidents and absurdities, for it sometimes happens that two people jump toward each other at the same time so that they encounter each other only in midair and after taking all that trouble they are just as far apart, one from the other, as they were before changing places.

XIII. This is by no means strange, because in actual fact the bridges to each other we cross so beautifully and festively are not *in* us, but rather behind us, exactly as in the landscapes of Fra Bartolomeo or Leonardo. Life truly does gather to a point in individual personalities. But between peak and peak the footpath runs through broad valleys.

XIV. When two or three people come together, that does not automatically mean they are with each other. They are like marionettes whose strings lie in different hands. Only when *one* hand guides them all do they have something in common, which can compel them to bow to the ground or start clobbering each other. And a person's power too resides there, in a single reigning hand that holds the ends of all the strings.

XV. They find each other only in the common hour, in the common storm, in the one room where they encounter each other. Only when a background lies behind them do they start to interact with each other. After all, they have to have a *single* home to appeal to. They have to show each other their valid credentials at the same time, the passports they carry

welche Alle den Sinn und das Insiegel desselben Fürsten enthalten.

XVI. Sei es das Singen einer Lampe oder die Stimme des Sturms, sei es das Atmen des Abends oder das Stöhnen des Meeres, das dich umgiebt – immer wacht hinter dir eine breite Melodie, aus tausend Stimmen gewoben, in der nur da und dort dein Solo Raum hat. Zu wissen, *wann Du einzufallen hast*, das ist das Geheimnis deiner Einsamkeit: wie es die Kunst des wahren Verkehres ist: aus den hohen Worten sich fallen lassen in die eine gemeinsame Melodie.

XVII. Wenn die Heiligen des Marco Basaiti sich etwas anzuvertrauen hätten außer ihrem seligen Nebeneinandersein, sie würden sich nicht vorn im Bild, drin sie wohnen, ihre schmalen, sanften Hände reichen. Sie würden sich zurückziehen, gleich klein werden und tief im lauschenden Land über die winzigen Brücken zueinander kommen.

XVIII. Wir vorn sind ganz ebenso. Segnende Sehnsüchte. Unsere Erfüllungen geschehen weit in leuchtenden Hintergründen. Dort ist Bewegung und Wille. Dort spielen die Historien, deren dunkle Überschriften wir sind. Dort ist unser Vereinen und unser Abschiednehmen, Trost und Trauer. Dort *sind* wir, während wir im Vordergrunde kommen und gehen.

XIX. Erinnere dich an Menschen, die du beisammen fandest, ohne daß sie eine gemeinsame Stunde um sich hatten. Zum Beispiel Verwandte, die sich im Sterbezimmer einer wirklich geliebten Person begegnen. Da lebt die eine in dieser, die andere in jener tiefen Erinnerung. Ihre Worte gehen aneinander vorbei, ohne daß sie von einander wissen. Ihre Hände verfehlen sich in der ersten Verwirrung. – Bis der Schmerz hinter ihnen breit wird. Sie setzen sich hin, senken die Stirnen und schweigen. Es rauscht über ihnen wie ein Wald. Und sie sind einander nahe, wie nie vorher.

with them, all of which contain the sign and seal of the same prince.

XVI. Whether it be the singing of a lamp or the voice of a storm, whether it be the breath of an evening or the groan of the ocean – whatever surrounds you, a broad melody always wakes behind you, woven out of a thousand voices, where there is room for your own solo only here and there. To know *when you need to join in*: that is the secret of your solitude: just as the art of true interactions with others is to let yourself fall away from high words into a single common melody.

XVII. If the saints of Marco Basaiti had had anything to confide to each other aside from their holy proximity side by side, they would not reach out their thin, soft hands up at the front of the pictures they live in. They would pull back, shrink to the same size, and, deep in the listening countryside, approach each other across the tiny bridges.

XVIII. We in front are exactly the same. Sanctifying desires. Our fulfillments take place deep in the radiant backgrounds. There, in the background, is motion, and will. There play out the histories; we are only the dark headlines. There is our reconciliation and our leavetaking, our consolation and sorrow. There, we *are*, while here in the foreground we come and go.

XIX. Recall the groups of people you have come upon without a common hour enveloping them. For example, relatives who meet at the deathbed of someone they truly loved. One of them lives in this deep memory, the other in that. Their words pass each other by, knowing nothing of each other. Their hands miss each other at first, in the confusion. – Until the pain behind them broadens out. They sit down, sink their foreheads, and say nothing. There is a rustle above them, like a forest. They are close to each other, as never before.

XX. Sonst, wenn nicht ein schwerer Schmerz die Menschen gleich still macht, hört der eine mehr, der andere weniger von der mächtigen Melodie des Hintergrundes. Viele hören sie gar nicht mehr. Sie sind wie Bäume welche ihre Wurzeln vergessen haben und nun meinen, daß das Rauschen ihrer Zweige ihre Kraft und ihr Leben sei. Viele haben nicht Zeit sie zu hören. Sie dulden keine Stunde um sich. Das sind arme Heimatlose, die den Sinn des Daseins verloren haben. Sie schlagen auf die Tasten der Tage und spielen immer denselben monotonen verlorenen Ton.

XXI. Wollen wir also Eingeweihte des Lebens sein, müssen wir zweierlei bedenken:

Einmal die große Melodie, in der Dinge und Düfte, Gefühle und Vergangenheiten, Dämmerungen und Sehnsüchte mitwirken, –

und dann: die einzelnen Stimmen, welche diesen vollen Chor ergänzen und vollenden.

Und um ein Kunstwerk, heißt: Bild des tieferen Lebens, des mehr als heutigen, immer zu allen Zeiten möglichen Erlebens, zu begründen, wird es notwendig sein die beiden Stimmen, *die* einer betreffenden Stunde und *die* einer Gruppe von Menschen darin, in das richtige Verhältnis zu setzen und auszugleichen.

XXII. Zu diesem Zweck muß man die beiden Elemente der Lebensmelodie in ihren primitiven Formen erkannt haben; man muß aus den rauschenden Tumulten des Meeres den Takt des Wogenschlages ausschälen und aus dem Netzgewirr täglichen Gespräches die lebendige Linie gelöst haben, welche die anderen trägt. Man muß die reinen Farben nebeneinanderhalten um ihre Kontraste und Vertraulichkeiten kennenzulernen. Man muß das Viele vergessen haben, um des Wichtigen willen.

XXIII. Zwei Menschen, die in gleichem Grade leise sind, müssen nicht von der Melodie ihrer Stunden reden. Diese ist ihr an und für sich Gemeinsames. Wie ein brennender Altar ist

XX. In other cases, when there is no difficult, deep pain to make people equally silent, one of them will hear more of the powerful melody of the background, the other less. Many no longer hear it at all. They are like trees that have forgotten their roots and now think that the rustling of their branches is their power and their life. Many people don't have time to hear it. They are too impatient to allow an hour to envelop them. These poor, homeless people have lost the meaning of existence. They strike the keyboard of their days and play the same, monotonous, lost note over and over again.

XXI. If, then, we want to be initiates of life, we must keep two things in mind:

First, the great melody, in which things and scents, feelings and pasts, twilights and desires, all play their parts; –

and second: the individual voices which augment and complete this full chorus.

And to lay the foundation for a work of art – that is, an image of deeper life, of our more than daily, always possible experience – we have to put both voices, the voice of this hour and the voice of a group of people within that hour, into a proper relationship and balance them.

XXII. To do this, you have to have learned how to recognize both elements of this melody of life in their primitive forms; you have to have extracted the rhythm of the beating of the waves from the roaring tumult of the sea, freed the living line that carries others from the tangled snarl of daily conversation. You have to hold pure colors next to each other to acquaint yourself with their contrasts and intimate harmonies. You have to forget the many for the sake of what's important.

XXIII. Two people who are equally quiet must not talk about the melody of their hours. This melody, in and of itself, is what they have in common. Like a burning altar it stands between

sie zwischen ihnen und sie nähren die heilige Flamme fürchtig mit ihren seltenen Silben.

Setze ich diese beiden Menschen aus ihrem absichtlosen Sein auf die Bühne, so ist mir offenbar darum zu tun, zwei Liebende zu zeigen und zu erklären, warum sie selig sind. Aber auf der Szene ist der Altar unsichtbar und es weiß keiner sich die seltsamen Gesten der Opfernden zu erklären.

XXIV. Da giebt es nun zwei Auswege:

entweder die Menschen müssen sich erheben und mit vielen Worten und verwirrenden Gebärden zu sagen versuchen, was sie vorher lebten.

Oder:

ich ändere nichts an ihrem tiefen Tun und sage selbst diese Worte dazu:

Hier ist ein Altar, auf welchem eine heilige Flamme brennt. Ihren Glanz können Sie auf den Gesichtern dieser beiden Menschen bemerken.

XXV. Das Letztere erscheint mir einzig künstlerisch. Es geht nichts von dem Wesentlichen verloren; keine Vermengung der einfachen Elemente trübt die Reihe der Ereignisse, wenn ich den Altar, der die zwei Einsamen vereint, so schildere, daß Alle ihn sehen und an sein Vorhandensein glauben. Viel später wird es den Schauenden unwillkürlich werden, die flammende Säule zu sehen, und ich werde nichts Erläuterndes hinzu sagen müssen. Viel später.

XXVI. Aber das mit dem Altar ist nur ein Gleichnis, und ein sehr ungefähres obendrein. Es handelt sich darum, auf der Szene die gemeinsame Stunde, das worin die Personen zuworte kommen, auszudrücken. Dieses Lied, welches im Leben den tausend Stimmen des Tages oder der Nacht, dem Waldrauschen oder dem Uhrenticken und ihrem zögernden Stundenschlag überlassen bleibt, dieser breite Chor des Hintergrundes, der den Takt und Ton unserer Worte bestimmt, läßt sich auf der Bühne zunächst nicht mit den gleichen Mitteln begreiflich machen.

them and they feed its holy flame with reverence, with a few rare syllables.

Now if I put these two people on stage, imposing an artistic design on their mere being, then it would seem that my intention is to show two lovers and explain why they are so blessed. But in the theater, the altar is invisible and no one can understand the strange gestures of sacrifice they are making.

XXIV. There are two ways out of this dilemma:

Either the two people have to stand up and try to say, with a multitude of words and confusing gestures, what they used to simply live.

Or:

I change nothing in their deep actions and add these words myself:

Here is an altar, on which a holy flame is burning. You can see its light shining on the faces of these two people.

XXV. The latter approach seems to me to be the only artistic one. Nothing essential is lost; no confusion of the simple elements muddies the series of events, as long as I portray the altar that unifies these two solitary people in such a way that everyone can see it and believes in its presence. Much later, on their own, the spectators will come to see the fiery columns, and I won't need to say anything further by way of explanation. Much later.

XXVI. But this whole story of the altar is only an analogy, a parable, and a very inexact one. The important thing is to express on stage their common hour, that within which the two people come to speak. The song itself, which in life is left to the thousand voices of the day and of the night, the rustling of the forest or the ticking of the clock and its hesitant tolling of the hours – this general chorus of the background that determines the rhythm and the tones of our words – cannot yet be made comprehensible on stage by these means.

XXVII. Denn das was man ›Stimmung‹ nennt und was ja in neueren Stücken auch teilweise zu seinem Rechte kommt, ist doch nur ein erster unvollkommener Versuch, die Landschaft hinter Menschen, Worten und Winken durchschimmern zu lassen, wird von den Meisten überhaupt nicht bemerkt und kann um seiner leiseren Intimität willen überhaupt nicht von Allen bemerkt werden. Eine technische Verstärkung einzelner Geräusche oder Beleuchtungen wirkt lächerlich, weil sie aus tausend Stimmen eine einzelne zuspitzt, so daß die ganze Handlung an der einen Kante hängen bleibt.

XXVIII. Diese Gerechtigkeit gegen das breite Lied des Hintergrundes bleibt nur erhalten, wenn man es in seinem ganzen Umfange gelten läßt, was zunächst sowohl den Mitteln unserer Bühne, wie der Auffassung der mißtrauischen Menge gegenüber untunlich erscheint. – Das Gleichgewicht kann nur durch eine strenge Stilisierung erreicht werden. Wenn man nämlich die Melodie der Unendlichkeit auf denselben Tasten spielt, auf denen die Hände der Handlung ruhen, das heißt das Große und Wortlose zu den Worten herunterstimmt.

XXIX. Dieses ist nichts anderes als die Einführung eines Chors, der sich ruhig aufrollt hinter den lichten und flimmernden Gesprächen. Dadurch daß die Stille in ihrer ganzen Breite und Bedeutung fortwährend wirkt, erscheinen die Worte vorn als ihre natürlichen Ergänzungen, und es kann dabei eine geründete Darstellung des Lebensliedes erzielt werden, welche sonst schon durch die Unverwendbarkeit von Düften und dunklen Empfindungen auf der Bühne, ausgeschlossen schien.

XXX. Ich will ein ganz kleines Beispiel andeuten: –
Abend. Eine kleine Stube. Am Mitteltisch unter der Lampe sitzen zwei Kinder einander gegenüber, ungern über ihre Bücher geneigt. Sie sind beide weit – weit. Die Bücher verdecken ihre Flucht. Dann und wann rufen sie sich an, um sich nicht in dem weiten Wald ihrer Träume zu verlieren. Sie erleben in der engen Stube bunte und phantastische Schicksale. Sie kämpfen und

XXVII. Because what people call "atmosphere" – which does come into its own somewhat in recent plays – is really just a first, incomplete attempt to let the landscape behind people, behind words and gestures, shimmer through. The majority don't even notice it, and because of its soft intimacy it will never be possible for everyone to notice it. A technical amplification of individual sounds or lighting effects would be ridiculous, because it intensifies a single voice from among the thousands so that the plot of the whole play is left hanging from a single corner.

XXVIII. You can do justice to the general song of the background only if you let it work in its entirety, and for the time being this seems to be impracticable, due to both the means of our stagecraft and the ideas that the suspicious theater-going masses hold dear. – Equilibrium can be achieved only through a strict stylization. If, namely, you play the melody of infinity on the same keyboard that the hands of the plot rest upon, if you tune the great and wordless down to the words.

XXIX. This process is nothing more or less than the introduction of a chorus that unfolds calmly behind the light, fluttering dialogues. The silence, by working incessantly in its whole breadth and significance, makes the words in front appear as what naturally completes it, and in this way a rounded presentation of the song of life can be achieved, which otherwise, since odors and dark sensations cannot be used onstage, seems impossible.

XXX. Let me sketch out a very small example: –

Evening. A small room. At the dining table, under a lamp, two children sit across from each other, reluctantly bent over their books. They are both far away – far away. The books conceal their flight. Now and then they call to each other, so that they won't lose themselves in the enormous forest of their dreams. They live out colorful, fantastic destinies in this narrow

siegen. Kommen heim und heiraten. Lehren ihre Kinder Helden sein. Sterben wohl gar.

Ich bin so eigenwillig, das für Handlung zu halten!

XXXI. Aber was ist diese Szene ohne das Singen der hellen altmodischen Hängelampe, ohne das Atmen und Stöhnen der Möbel, ohne den Sturm um das Haus. Ohne diesen ganzen dunklen Hintergrund, durch welchen sie die Fäden ihrer Fabeln ziehen. Wie anders würden die Kinder im Garten träumen, anders am Meer, anders auf der Terrasse eines Palastes. Es ist nicht gleichgültig, ob man in Seide oder in Wolle stickt. Man muß wissen, daß sie in dem gelben Canevas dieses Stubenabends die paar ungelenken Linien ihres Maeandermusters unsicher wiederholen.

XXXII. Ich denke nun daran, die ganze Melodie so wie die Knaben sie hören, erklingen zu lassen. Eine stille Stimmemuß sie über der Szene schweben, und auf ein unsichtbares Zeichen fallen die winzigen Kinderstimmen ein und treiben hin, während der breite Strom durch die enge Abendstube weiterrauscht von Unendlichkeit zu Unendlichkeit.

XXXIII. Solcher Szenen weiß ich viele und breitere. Je nach ausdrücklicher, ich meine allseitiger Stilisierung oder vorsichtiger Andeutung derselben, findet der Chor auf der Szene selbst seinen Raum und wirkt dann auch durch seine wachsame Gegenwart, oder sein Anteil beschränkt sich auf die Stimme, die, breit und unpersönlich, aus dem Brauen der gemeinsamen Stunde steigt. In jedem Fall wohnt auch in ihr, wie im antiken Chor, das weisere Wissen; nicht weil sie urteilt über das Geschehen der Handlung, sondern weil sie die Basis ist, aus der jenes leisere Lied sich auslöst und in deren Schooß es endlich schöner zurückfällt.

XXXIV. Die stilisierte, also unrealistische Darstellung halte ich in diesem Fall nur für einen Übergang; denn auf der Bühne

room. They fight battles; win victories. Return home and marry. Teach their children to be heroes. Even die.

I am unconventional enough to consider that a plot!

XXXI. But what is this scene without the singing of the bright, old-fashioned hanging lamp, without the breathing and the groaning of the furniture, without the storm raging outside the house. Without this whole dark background, through which the children draw the threads of their fables. How differently they would dream in the garden, differently again by the sea, differently again on a palace terrace. It is not the same thing to embroider on silk and on wool. The audience has to know that the children are unsteadily repeating the two clumsy lines of their meander pattern on the yellow canvas of *this* evening in *this* room.   *particular / specifics*

XXXII. What matters is to let the whole melody ring out the way the boys hear it. A silent voice has to hover over the scene, and at an invisible sign the tiny voices of the children enter and drift there while the broader current surges onward through the narrow evening room from infinity to infinity.

XXXIII. I know many such scenes, and broader ones. Depending on whether the scene is explicit, I mean comprehensively stylized, or only cautiously hinted at, the chorus will either find its place in the scene itself and its vigilant presence will do its work, or else it will be confined to the role of a voice which, broad and impersonal, arises from the common hour gathered around. In any case, in this voice, as in the chorus of classical drama, resides a wiser wisdom: not because this voice passes judgment on what happens in the plot, but because it is the foundation from which that soft song is released and back into whose lap it eventually, beautifully falls.

XXXIV. I consider this stylized, in other words unrealistic, presentation to be only a transition, because what is most welcome

wird immer diejenige Kunst am willkommensten sein, welche lebensähnlich und in diesem äußeren Sinne ›wahr‹ ist. Aber dieses gerade ist der Weg zu einer selbst sich vertiefenden, innerlichen Wahrheit: die primitiven Elemente zu erkennen und zu verwenden. Hinter einer ernsten Erfahrung wird man die begriffenen Grundmotive freier und eigenwilliger brauchen lernen und damit auch wieder dem realistischen, dem zeitlich Wirklichen näher kommen. Es wird aber nicht dasselbe sein wie vorher.

XXXV. Diese Bemühungen erscheinen mir notwendig, weil sonst die Erkenntnis der feineren Gefühle, die eine lange und ernste Arbeit sich errang, im Lärm der Bühne ewig verloren gehen würde. Und das ist schade. Von der Bühne her kann, wenn es tendenzlos und unbetont geschieht, das neue Leben verkündet, das heißt auch denen vermittelt werden, die nicht aus eigenem Drang und eigener Kraft seine Gebärden lernen. Sie sollen nicht bekehrt werden von der Szene her. Aber sie sollen wenigstens erfahren: das giebt es in unserer Zeit, eng neben uns. Das ist schon Glückes genug.

XXXVI. Denn es ist fast von der Bedeutung einer Religion, dieses Einsehen: daß man, sobald man einmal die Melodie des Hintergrundes gefunden hat, nicht mehr ratlos ist in seinen Worten und dunkel in seinen Entschlüssen. Es ist eine sorglose Sicherheit in der einfachen Überzeugung, Teil einer Melodie zu sein, also einen bestimmten Raum zu Recht zu besitzen und eine bestimmte Pflicht an einem breiten Werke zu haben, in dem der Geringste ebensoviel wertet wie der Größte. Nicht überzählig zu sein, ist die erste Bedingung der bewußten und ruhigen Entfaltung.

XXXVII. Aller Zwiespalt und Irrtum kommt davon her, daß die Menschen das Gemeinsame *in* sich, statt in den Dingen *hinter* sich, im Licht, in der Landschaft im Beginn und im Tode, suchen. Sie verlieren dadurch sich selbst und gewinnen nichts dafür. Sie vermischen sich, weil sie sich doch nicht vereinen

on stage is always the art that is closest to life, and in that external sense "true." Precisely this approach, however – to recognize and use the primitive elements – is the path to a deepening, inward truth. After serious experience with these basic motifs, we will understand them and learn how to use them more freely and unconventionally, and thus also return closer to realism, to what is true in time. But it will not be the same truth as before. *truth of that specific moment*

XXXV. These efforts seem necessary to me, because otherwise the finer feelings which we come to know only by long and serious work will be lost forever in the noise of the stage. That would be a shame. A new life can be proclaimed, and thus also imparted, from the stage, when it is done without bias or emphasis, to those who would not learn how to perform that life's gestures from their own need and with their own power. The play doesn't need to convert them. But they should at least experience that there is this life, in our time, close beside us. That would be happiness enough.

XXXVI. It has an almost religious importance, this seeing: this recognition that the moment you have found the melody of the background you are no longer helpless in your words and vague in your decisions. There is a security, without worries, in the simple conviction that you are a part of a melody, that you rightfully possess a certain place and have a certain duty to a broad, general work in which the smallest part is worth just as much as the greatest. Not to be superfluous – that is the first prerequisite for a calm and conscious unfolding.

XXXVII. All conflict, all error, comes from the fact that people look for what they have in common *in* themselves, not in the things *behind* them, in the light, in the landscape in the beginning, and in death. They lose themselves and gain nothing in return. They mingle with each other because they cannot truly

können. Sie halten sich aneinander und können doch nicht sicheren Fuß fassen, weil sie beide schwankend und schwach sind; und in diesem gegenseitigen Sich-stützen-wollen geben sie ihre ganze Stärke aus, so daß nach außen hin auch nicht die Ahnung eines Wellenschlages fühlbar wird.

XXXVIII. Jedes Gemeinsame setzt aber eine Reihe unterschiedener einsamer Wesen voraus. Vor ihnen war es einfach ein Ganzes ohne jegliche Beziehung, so vor sich hin. Es war weder arm noch reich. Mit dem Augenblick, wo verschiedene seiner Teile der mütterlichen Einheit entfremden, tritt es in Gegensatz zu ihnen; denn sie entwickeln sich von ihm fort. Aber es läßt sie doch nicht aus der Hand. Wenn die Wurzel auch nicht von den Früchten weiß, sie nährt sie doch.

XXXIX. Und wie Früchte sind wir. Hoch hangen wir in seltsam verschlungenen Ästen und viele Winde geschehen uns. Was wir besitzen, das ist unsere Reife und Süße und Schönheit. Aber die Kraft dazu strömt in *einem* Stamm aus einer über Welten hin weit gewordenen Wurzel in uns Alle. Und wenn wir für ihre Macht zeugen wollen, so müssen wir sie jeder brauchen in unserem einsamsten Sinn. Je mehr Einsame, desto feierlicher, ergreifender und mächtiger ist ihre Gemeinsamkeit.

XXXX. Und gerade die Einsamsten haben den größten Anteil an der Gemeinsamkeit. Ich sagte früher, daß der eine mehr, der andere weniger von der breiten Lebensmelodie vernimmt; dem entsprechend fällt ihm auch eine kleinere oder geringere Pflicht in dem großen Orchester zu. Derjenige, welcher die ganze Melodie vernähme, wäre der Einsamste und Gemeinsamste zugleich. Denn er würde hören, was Keiner hört, und doch nur weil er in seiner *Vollendung* begreift, was die anderen dunkel und lückenhaft erlauschen.

come together. They cling to each other and cannot truly find their feet because both people are swaying and weak; they expend all their strength in this mutual wanting to prop each other up, so that, from the outside, not even a tiny tidal rhythm can be perceived.

XXXVIII. Anything had in common, however, presupposes a range of different solitary beings. Before their differentiation, there was simply a whole, without any relationships, existing for itself. It was neither poor nor rich. At the moment when its various parts split off from the maternal unity, they become opposed to what they had in common; they develop away from it. But it doesn't really let them go. Even if the root knows nothing of the fruits, it nourishes them nevertheless.

XXXIX. And we are like fruits. We hang high on strangely jagged branches and suffer many winds. What we possess is our ripeness and sweetness and beauty. But the power to attain these possessions courses into us all through *one* trunk, from a broad root stretching across whole worlds. If we would bear witness to its power, we must use that power, every one of us, in our most individual, solitary sense. The more solitary people there are, the more solemn and moving and powerful their commonality.

XXXX. It is precisely the most solitary people who have the greatest share of commonality. I said earlier that one person perceives more, another less, of the general melody of life; each person is assigned a correspondingly smaller or narrower task in the great orchestra. The one who could perceive the whole melody would be most solitary and most in the community at once. He would hear what no one hears, and only because he understands, in his *completion*, what the others overhear vaguely and full of gaps.

[Haï-Kaï]

C'est pourtant plus lourd de porter des fruits que des fleurs /
Mais ce n'est pas un arbre qui parle –
c'est un amoureux.

Entre ses vingt fards
elle cherche un pot plein :
devenu pierre.

Haiku

I

Still, fruits are much heavier than flowers . . .
But it's not a tree that speaks these words,
it's a lover.

II

Among her twenty jars of make-up
she looks for an empty one:
turned to stone.

Sie sind auf Seiten dessen,
was uns vermehrt, unermessen,
brauchen nicht Nahrung und Wein;
doch, daß sie's tastend erkannten,
macht sie uns zu Verwandten, –
und die Speise wird rein
von der nötigen Tötung:
sie verlöschen die Rötung
alles tierischen Bluts.
Schaffen uns Künste der Küche
Lockung und Wohlgerüche,
ihre Reinigung tuts.

III

Kennst du das, daß durch das Laubwerk Scheine
fallen in den Schatten, und es weht ...
: wie dann in des fremden Lichtes Reine,
kaum geschaukelt, blau und einzeln, eine
hohe Glockenblume steht:

Also bist du, bei den Toten, immer
in ein ausgespartes Licht gestellt,
langsam schwankend ... Andre leiden schlimmer.
Und in deinem unbenutzten Schimmer
spielt der Überfluß der Unterwelt.

VII

DAS (NICHT VORHANDENE) KINDERGRAB MIT DEM BALL

I

Von diesen Kreuzen keins,
nicht Englein, hölzern und zinnern,

They are on the side
of that which nourishes us, immeasurable;
they don't need bread and wine;
still, now that they've tried
it, tasted,
we and they are related –
and the supper is purified
of its needful death:
they wash out the red
of the animal blood.
The kitchen's arts may tempt us
and make the food smell good
but *their* cleansing does it.

III

You know how the shimmer of light falls through the leaves
and into the shadows, and the wind blows? . . .
: how then in the strange light's purity,
lightly rocked back and forth, blue and solitary,
a tall bell-flower stands:

So too are you, with the dead,
always set where the light is left,
slowly wavering . . . Others suffer more.
And in your unused glow
there plays the underworld's overflow.

IV
(NONEXISTENT) CHILD'S GRAVE WITH BALL

I

Not one of these crosses, nor all
of these little angels in wood or metal –

dürften an dich erinnern
als kleines Ein-mal-eins

des Tods, den du selber dir deutest:
sondern, es liege der Ball,
den du, zu werfen, dich freutest,
– einfacher Niederfall –

in einem goldenen Netz
über der tieferen Truhe.
Sein Bogen und, nun, seine Ruhe
befolgen dasselbe Gesetz.

2

Du warsts imstand und warfst ihn weit hinein
in die Natur; sie nahm ihn wie den ihren
und ließ getrost sein Etwas-wärmer-sein
in ihren sichern Räumen sich verlieren.

Dann kam er wieder, himmlisch abgekühlt:
wie hast du, ihm entgegen, froh beklommen,
das Übermaß in seinem Wiederkommen
mit allem Übermaß zugleich gefühlt.

3

Wir werfen dieses Ding, das uns gehört,
in das Gesetz aus unserm dichten Leben,
wo immer wieder Wurf und Sturz sich stört.

Da schwebt es hin und zieht in reinem Strich
die Sehnsucht aus, die wir ihm mitgegeben –,
sieht uns zurückgeblieben, wendet sich
und meint, im Fall, der zunimmt, uns zu heben.

none of this basic arithmetic
of death can be your memorial.

The problem of death, you have solved it
on your own. But if there were a ball
lying in its golden net
– simply let fall –

atop the deep-set chest,
the ball you loved to throw:
Its arc and now its rest
would both follow the same law.

2

You were in a position to throw and you threw
it deep into Nature; she took it in
as her own, consoled, and let it lose
its extra warmth in her certain skies.

Then it returned, cooled down by heaven:
how happily anxious you felt when you saw it;
the extravagance of its return
was every extravagance at once.

3

We take this thing that belongs to us and throw it
into the law and out of our thick-packed lives
unsettled again and again by throw and plummet.

It floats up, drawing out in a pure line
the longing we have given it, our desire –
it sees us left behind and turns, and thinks,
in its falling ever faster, to lift us higher.

VIII

Das Spiel, da man sich an die Bäume stellt,
um mit einander rasch den Platz zu tauschen:
wars nicht ein letztes Suchen und Belauschen
der einmal innerlich bewohnten Welt?

Sie sprangen fast wie aus den Bäumen vor:
erregte Mädchen in gekreuzter Helle ...
Und wer im Wechseln seinen Platz verlor,
der war der Liebesgott und ohne Stelle.

Die Mitte, die nach allen Seiten schreckt,
die Wahl die zuckt, das Zücken aller Schritte –,
und wie von Göttlicherem angesteckt,
war jede innen beides: Baum und Mitte.

V

That game where you stand against a tree
and dash to trade places with each other:
wasn't that one last listening in
on the lost world we once lived within?

They leapt right out of the trees almost,
excited girls in criss-crossed light . . .
And the girl who lost her place in the trade
was the god of love, without a post.

The center, startled in all directions,
the quivering choice, the tug of the footsteps – ;
in every girl, as if set on fire
by something godlike: both tree and center.

Daß einer auf seinem angeborenen Platz aufsänge, sei es auch hinter einer Maschine oder am Pflug (was ja sogar eine recht vergünstigte Lage wäre!), ist natürlich in der Ordnung; andererseits aber wäre es falsch, überall das »métier« gelten zu lassen, um den künstlerisch Schreibenden (ich vermeide das abscheuliche: »Schriftsteller«) von dem seinen zu verdrängen. Niemand dächte daran, einen Seiler, Schreiner oder Schuster von ihrem Handwerk weg »ins Leben« zu stoßen, damit sie bessere Seiler, Schreiner und Schuhmacher seien; auch den Musiker, den Maler, den Skulpteur ließe man eher bei dem Ihrigen gewähren. Nur bei dem Schreibenden scheint das Handwerk so gering, so von vornherein *gekonnt* (Schreiben kann jeder), daß manche [...] der Meinung waren, der damit Beschäftigte gerate sofort ins leere Spielen, wenn man ihn zu sehr mit seinem métier allein lasse! Aber welcher Irrtum! Schreiben zu können ist, weiß Gott, nicht minder »schweres Handwerk«, um so mehr, als das Material der anderen Künste von vornherein von dem täglichen Gebrauch abgerückt ist, während des Dichters Aufgabe sich steigert um die seltsame Verpflichtung, *sein* Wort von den Worten des bloßen Umgangs und der Verständigung gründlich, wesentlich zu unterscheiden. *Kein* Wort im Gedicht (ich meine hier jedes »*und*« oder »*der*«, »*die*«, »*das*«) ist *identisch* mit dem gleichlautenden Gebrauchs- und Konversations-Worte; die reinere Gesetzmäßigkeit, das große Verhältnis, die Konstellation, die es im Vers oder in künstlerischer Prosa einnimmt, verändert es bis in den Kern seiner Natur, macht es nutzlos, unbrauchbar für den bloßen Umgang, unberührbar und bleibend: ...

74

On the Poet's Material

Naturally, it makes sense to send your song aloft from your native place, even if it be behind a machine or a plow (which would, in fact, be a much improved situation!); on the other hand, it's wrong to give someone's background precedence over everything in order to force the person who writes artistically (I avoid the odious word "author") away from his true occupation. No one would think to elbow a carpenter, a cobbler, or a cooper away from his craft out "into the world" so that he might be a better carpenter, cobbler, or cooper; musicians, painters, and sculptors too are mostly left alone with their work. Only with someone whose work is writing does the craft, the manual labor, seem so negligible, so *mastered* in advance (everyone can write!), that people think he would immediately descend into empty game-playing if left too much alone with his occupation. But what a mistake! To be able to write is, God knows, no less "heavy labor," especially since the raw material of the other arts comes already dissociated from daily use while the poet's task includes a strange additional duty: that of differentiating *his* word, fundamentally and essentially, from the words of mere interaction and communication. *No* word in a poem (and here I mean every last "and" and "the" too) is *the same* as the identical-sounding word in conversation and ordinary use. The word's purer accordance with the law, its grand interrelations and proportion, the constellation that it occupies in a line of poetry or piece of artistic prose changes it, down to the core of its nature, and makes it useless, unusable for mere interaction, untouchable and lasting.

Ehe

Sie ist traurig, lautlos und allein.
Sieh, sie leidet. Deine Nächte legten
sich auf ihre leisen leicht erregten
Nächte wie ein stürzendes Gestein.

Hundertmal in deiner dumpfen Gier
warst du ihr Vergeuder und Vergifter;
aber daß du einmal wie ein Stifter
still und dunkel knietest neben ihr
macht dich männlich und geht aus von dir.

Marriage

She is sad, wordless and alone.
See how she suffers. And then your nights
descend on her quiet, restless nights
like a plummeting stone.

A hundred times, in your dull lust, you
have squandered her and poisoned her;
but once, like a medieval donor,
you darkly, silently knelt by her:
this makes you a man and goes forth from you.

[Aufzeichnung]

Wieviel Zeit hatte er gebraucht, um seinen ältesten, verhängnisvollsten Fehler einzusehen: daß er Liebe, die auf ihn ausging, wie seine eigene Angelegenheit nahm, obwohl sie doch die entfernteste war, vielleicht überhaupt keine, indifferent wie der Zahnschmerz eines Fremden. Warum in aller Welt hatte er sich dann immer veranlaßt gefühlt, den Zahnarzt zu spielen? Statt einfach nicht hinzusehen, nicht zu wissen. Es wäre eine herrliche Keuschheit seiner Natur gewesen, nicht zu verstehen, daß die anderen liebten, es einfach nicht zu verstehen. Aber auf ihn stürzte sich der Einfluß selbst aus dem möglichen Aufblick einer Vorübergehenden, bewog, rührte, verführte ihn. Und was ihn schließlich zu etwas Starrem, Anstehenden machte, das war die Gewalt so vieler ihn meinender, von ihm unterhaltener, unabgelehnter, halb hingenommener Gefühle. Alle Strömungen gingen auf ihn zu; er konnte mit keiner Empfindung aus sich heraus wider ihre Flut. Liebende schlossen ihn von allen Seiten ein. Er war in der Lage eines Gottes, der keinen Ausweg mehr hat auf der von ihm überfüllten Welt, dem nur die Senkrechte bleibt: Höllensturz oder Himmelfahrt. Daher seine Erfahrung, ein Gestorbener zu sein, da ihm alles Menschliche abgeschnitten war und er doch nicht des Göttlichen mächtig wurde.

Wenn sie ihm Blumen brachten, viel zu viele, zu schwere, übertriebene Blumen, so wünschte er ein Grab zu sein, um nicht die Mühe zu haben, sie zu ordnen und zu erhalten. Und sie kamen auch wie zu einem Grab zu ihm, dem Wehrlosen, der sich Rührung und Hingabe so schamlos gefallen ließ. Hatte er alle Jahre seines Lebens verbracht, ohne hart zu sein? Er entschloß sich, es zu werden in seinem achtunddreißigsten Jahr. Ändern, sagte er, ändern. In der Zeit, da seine ganze Natur unermeßlich danach begehrte zu lieben, sah er schmerzlich ein, daß er den Gegenstand seiner Liebe nicht finden würde, solange er gegen die, die ihn zu lieben meinten, empfänglich und nachgiebig war. Diese Gesichter, die sich zu ihm drängten, aufgeschlagen, verstellten ihm den Ausblick auf das scheue,

In His Thirty-Eighth Year

How much time it has taken him to see through his oldest, most fatal mistake! Always taking the love that shone upon him as his own concern, even though it was in fact the most distant thing in the world from him, maybe nothing whatsoever, indifferent, like a stranger's toothache. Why in the world had he always felt obliged to play the dentist? Instead of simply looking elsewhere, not acknowledging it. It would have been a marvellous chastity in his nature not to understand that others loved, simply not to understand it. But he felt it rushing in even from a woman passing by who happened to look up at him: it moved him, touched him, seduced him. And what finally made him into something rigid and inflexible was the violence of so many feelings directed at him, which he entertained, half accepted or at least refused to decline. All these currents came at him; he could not push back against the flood with any of the feelings or emotions coming from himself. Lovers hemmed him in on all sides. He was in the situation of a god with no way out anywhere in the world he has filled to overflowing; only vertical motion remains for him: a descent into Hell or ascension to Heaven. This is the source of his feeling that he is a dead man, since everything human has been cut away from him and yet he has not attained to divine power.

When they brought him flowers – many too many, too heavy, exaggerated flowers – he wished he were a grave so as not to have the trouble of keeping the flowers and arranging them. And they even came to him as though to a grave, to something defenseless that shamelessly accepts emotion and devotion. Had he really spent all the years of his life without being hard? He decided to become hard in his thirty-eighth year. Change, he told himself, change. In the days when his whole nature had an infinite longing to love, he had realized, painfully, that he would never find the object of his love as long as he stayed receptive and yielding to those who thought they loved him. These faces crowding in on him like open books blocked his

gesenkte Gesicht der fremden Geliebten. Die Ahnung ihrer Züge erlosch in ihm über der Deutlichkeit derer, die gekommen waren, ihn zu lieben. Er wurde irre. Er stand an einer Straßenecke und wußte sie nicht mehr. Er wartete und wußte sie nicht mehr. Er konnte nicht mehr träumen: alle seine Zukunft war vorüber.

view of the shy, lowered face of his unknown beloved. His vague idea of her features was extinguished by the clarity of the faces of those who had come to love him. He lost his way. He stood on a street corner and no longer knew her. He waited, and no longer knew her. He could no longer dream: his whole future had come to an end.

Das Testament

Glaube nicht, Künstler, daß deine Prüfung in der Arbeit sei. Du bist nicht, wofür du dich giebst und als den der oder jener dich nehmen mag, weil er's nicht besser weiß, solang sie dir nicht so ganz Natur geworden ist, daß du gar nicht anders *kannst*, als dich bewähren in ihr. So arbeitend bist du der meisterhaft geworfene Speer: Gesetze empfangen dich aus der Hand der Werferin und stürzen mit dir ins Ziel. – Was wäre gesicherter als dein Flug?

Deine Prüfung aber sei, daß du nicht immer geworfen bist. Daß die Speerspielerin Einsamkeit dich nicht wählt, lange nicht, daß sie dich vergißt. Das ist die Zeit der Versuchungen, wenn du dich ungebraucht, unfähig fühlst. (Als ob es nicht genügend Beschäftigung wäre, bereit zu sein!) Dann, wenn du nicht sehr schwer daliegst, üben sich die Zerstreuungen an dir und versuchen, wie du anders zu verwenden sein möchtest. Als Stab eines Blinden, als eine unter den Stangen eines Gitters oder als der Gleichgewichtsstock eines Seiltänzers. Oder sie sind's imstand und pflanzen dich ein ins Erdreich des Schicksals, daß dir das Wunder der Jahreszeiten geschähe und du triebest vielleicht grüne Blätter des Glücks . . .

Oh dann, eherner: liege schwer.
Sei Speer. Sei Speer. Sei Speer!

* * *

In der Militärschule sah ich es zuerst ein; später im Infanteristenrock. Und nun wieder: wie doch jeder Kreatur gewissermaßen nur jenes Schwere widerfährt, das auf der Ebene ihrer Kräfte liegt, wenn auch diese dann oft bei weitem übersteigend.

Wir aber, die wir in dem unfaßlichen Durchschnittspunkt so vieler verschiedener und einander widersprechenden Umwelten stehen, kommen in die Lage, plötzlich von einem Schweren überfallen zu sein, das mit unserem Können und seiner Übung in keiner Weise zusammenhängt: einem *fremden* Schweren.

From Testament

Do not think, artist, that work is what tests you. You are not what you pretend to be, not what this or that person who doesn't know any better takes you to be, – not until your work has become your true nature so completely that you *cannot* do anything but prove your worth in it. Then, when you work like that, you are the masterfully thrown spear: laws receive you from the hand of the spear-thrower and plunge with you into the target. – What could be more certain than your flight?

What tests you, though, is that you are not always thrown. That Solitude the spear-thrower does not choose you; that years go by, she forgets you. That is the time of temptations, when you feel yourself unused, unable. (As though keeping yourself ready were not work enough!) Then, while you lie there, not particularly heavily, distractions play upon you and try to use you differently from how you want to be used. Try to use you as a blind man's staff, as one of the bars in a grille, as a balancing pole for a tightrope walker. Or they succeed in planting you in the soil of fate, so that you too undergo the miracle of the seasons and put forth, perhaps, little green buds of happiness. . . .

> Then, iron one, lie heavy. Do not fear:
> Be spear. Be spear. Be spear!

* * *

I observed it first in military school; then later in my infantry uniform, and now once more: how, truly, the only difficulty to befall every creature is the one that lies at the level of his powers, even if it often far exceeds those powers.

But we, standing at the incomprehensible point of intersection of so many different, contradictory environments, encounter the situation where a difficulty attacks us which has nothing whatsoever to do with our abilities and what we are prepared for: a difficulty alien to us.

(Wann wäre dem Schwan eine der Prüfungen des Löwen zugemutet? Wie geriete ein Stück Fischschicksal in die Fassung der Fledermaus –, oder der Schrecken eines Pferds an die verdauende Schlange?)

Ich glaube deshalb, daß ich schon als Kind nie um etwas anderes gebetet habe, als um *mein* Schweres, daß mir das meine geschähe, nicht aus Versehen das des Tischlers oder des Lohnkutschers oder des Soldaten, denn in meinem Schwersten will ich mich erkennen.

Nur infolge der Verwirrung im unabgegrenzten, nach allen Seiten neugierigen Menschlichen, die es mit sich brachte, daß jedem *alles* zustoßen konnte, war es möglich, daß der Untergang in Verruf geriet. Wie vertraulich ist er, wenn man ihm im eigenen, im leidenschaftlich Gekonnten begegnet!

* * *

Nichts soll aus jener schweren ›fremden‹ Heimsuchung aufbewahrt sein, die mich, da ich eben hier begonnen hatte, das Werk meiner Besinnung zu tun, eines Morgens um vier (es war noch Nacht, und ein kalter Regen fiel in der Finsternis) fort und nach G. trieb. Niemand wird je mehr davon erfahren, als was ich in stiller Rechenschaft diesen Blättern anvertraue. Aber ehe ich das kleine Taschenbuch in blauem Leder verbrenne, das ich damals mit auf die Reise nahm, will ich über seinen Zustand Bericht ablegen. Kaum drei Seiten darin sind beschrieben; aber was neben zwei Adressen diese Seiten dicht ausfüllt, macht mir die vielen, vielen leeren Blätter so unheimlich, daß ich sie, wie angesteckt und verseucht, mit ins Feuer werfe. Ich schreibe hier, ohne das mindeste zu verändern, eines nach dem anderen, ehe ich sie vernichte, die sinnlosen Worte ab, in denen sich mein damals fähiger Geist zersetzte, da ein ›fremdes‹ Schweres plötzlich wie eine scharfe Säure über ihn ausgegossen war.

(Aus dem zerstörten Taschenbuche:)

(Oben am Rande, das Wort:) Nachtmahr –,

(When would a swan be expected to pass one of the tests of the lion? How could any part of a fish's fate disturb the composure of the bat? – or the horse's terrible fright reach the digesting snake?)

So I believe that, even as a child, I never prayed for anything other than my difficult thing, prayed that *mine* happen to me, not, by some oversight, the carpenter's difficulties or the coachman's or the soldier's; it is in my own most difficult thing that I want to recognize myself.

Only as a result of the confusion of mankind, free of limits and curious in all directions – which brought with it the fact that *everything* can happen to everyone – could it become disreputable to be defeated. What a familiar friend defeat is when we encounter him in what is ours, in what we have passionately mastered!

* * *

Let nothing be preserved of that difficult, "alien" disaster which descended upon me and drove me forth, to G., one morning at four (it was still night; a cold rain fell in the darkness), when I had just begun the work of coming to my senses. No one will ever learn anything else from me except the silent account I entrust to these pages. But before I burn the small blue leather notebook that I took with me then, on that journey, I want to set down this report of its condition. Barely three of its pages contain writing, but what thickly covers those pages, besides two addresses, makes the many, many empty pages so disturbing to me, so uncanny, that I am throwing them into the fire too, as though infected and contaminated. I transcribe here, without changing the least thing, one after the other, before I destroy them, the senseless words into which my once able spirit decomposed when an "alien" difficulty was suddenly poured over it like corrosive acid.

(From the destroyed notebook:)

(On the top edge, the word:) Nightmare

(dann Zahlen, ohne Ordnung, Additionen kleiner
sinnloser Posten, dann:)

›Silber Freude Rohheit Runde Loos Lieber
Aufguß Sand Weshalb Nimmer Achtung
Lauer Nieder Neid Vielfraß Seegen Sucht
Nager Weg Ast vertieft Zaun Sage Einfalt
Wespe Herz Kino (Kind) Trauer Taufall
Gerücht Ring Sanftmut Abend Wiege
Lebendige Speise Vogel Ähre Loos nicht
Taufstein Ärger Trübe Bunt Beifall
Wesen Saumtier Ätzung Hinweg Ausfall
Haartracht Zäune Taifun Ach Wiege Mai
Hartung Silber Nebel Wege Ruf Brief
Bote Busta Nota Auto Timgad Ufer
Raufe Trank Neuling Wink Oh Achse
Glanz Fink Steuer Sturm Stein Ribe
Johannisfeuer Dienst August Pose Possard
Nonne Neerung Spieß Spülung Heiter
Saum Kerbe Wesen genau Last Senke (?)
Griff Geifer Kralle Übung Nachtzug Eifer
Wüste Speer Taumel Einbruch Rage Lauf
Lebzelt Zittergras Nachmittag Überall Hun-
dert Heilung Hefe Wieburg Verschwender
König Dorn Stufe Ungut Ungelt Trauffe
Tragstein Trille Treubruch Scham Ost Fehr
Caseïn Kommer Kranz Bistum Beere
Bahre Bär Zwerch Zirpe Stempel Arg

Neue Seite:

Wiederkehr Liebling Taucher Vogelkopf
Angstschweiß Halsband Dornreif Wikuna
Ringband Lastkarrn Liebknecht Agnese
Terwin Garn Gast Rolle Brille Wille Schule
Thugut Marie Iffland Herzblut Wimmer
Zweibruck Feierabend Wendlandt Abstieg

(then numbers at random, little meaningless sums, then:)

"Silver Pleasure Roughness Rounded Lot Lover
Brew Sand Why Never Warning
Lurking Low Envy Glutton Blassing Longing
Gnawer Path Branch absorbed Fence Legend Innocence
Hornet Heart Film (Fille) Mourning Dewfall
Rumor Ring Gentleness Evening Cradle
Living Dish Bird Cornstalk Lot no
Baptistry Troubles Dull Colorful Applause
Creature Sumpter Cautery Away Omission
Hairstyle Fences Typhoon Ah Cradle May
Firstmonth Silver Mist Paths Call Letter
Messenger Busta Nota Auto Timgad Riverbank
Hayrack Potion Greenhorn Nod Oh Axis
Gleam Finch Taxes Tempest Stone Ribe
Midsummer Service August Pose Possard
Nun Eddy Skewer Flush Cheerful
Burden Kermis Creature precisely Weight Hollow (?)
Grip Slobber Talon Practice Night-Train Eager
Wasteland Spear Frenzy Break-In Fury Course
Honeycake Quaking-Grass Afternoon Everywhere Hun-
dred Healing Yeast Wieburg Spendthrift
King Thorn Step Unkind Excise Eaves
Keystone Warble Treachery Shame East Fehr
Casein Comer Circle Bishopric Berry
Bier Bear Dia Cicada Postmark Wicked

New page:

Return Favorite Diver Birdhead
Fearsweat Neckband Thornripe Vicuña
Ringband Wheelbarrow Liebknecht Agnese
Terwin Yarn Guest Roll Brill Will School
Virtu Marie Iffland Lifeblood Vintner
Doublebruck Holiday Wendland Downwards

Spur Spürung Neige Vierzug Zander Zaun-
gast Larde Feilitzsch Triefe Bestimmung
Nur Bast Brausen Ballast Nachtherz Eigen-
sinn sauber Urgast Billung bereitet
Saumzwang Niefeln Hieber Beherzung
Ichthüs Nomenclatur Beinung Richter
Regulus Galgen Wehrkraft Karde Spule
spielt langsam aber keine Musik reicht
an den Reigen Naumann‹

(Und drei Adressen.)

Trace Tracking Dregs Fourfold Pike-Perch Fence-
Guest Larde Hagglebag Blear Regulation
Only Bast Sprays Ballast Nightheart Ob-
stinacy clean Ur-Guest Proval preparedness
Burdenforce Swipe Thrasher Courage
Ichthyic Nomenclature Boneage Judge
Regulus Gallows Military Teasel Spool
plays slow but no music reaches
the roundelay Naumann"

(And three addresses.)

Komm du, du letzter, den ich anerkenne,
heilloser Schmerz im leiblichen Geweb:
wie ich im Geiste brannte, sieh, ich brenne
in dir; das Holz hat lange widerstrebt,
der Flamme, die du loderst, zuzustimmen,
nun aber nähr' ich dich und brenn in dir.
Mein hiesig Mildsein wird in deinem Grimmen
ein Grimm der Hölle nicht von hier.
Ganz rein, ganz planlos frei von Zukunft stieg
ich auf des Leidens wirren Scheiterhaufen,
so sicher nirgend Künftiges zu kaufen
um dieses Herz, darin der Vorrat schwieg.
Bin ich es noch, der da unkenntlich brennt?
Erinnerungen reiß ich nicht herein.
O Leben, Leben: Draußensein.
Und ich in Lohe. Niemand der mich kennt.

[Verzicht. Das ist nicht so wie Krankheit war
einst in der Kindheit. Aufschub. Vorwand um
größer zu werden. Alles rief und raunte.
Misch nicht in dieses was dich früh erstaunte]

(the last entry in Rilke's last notebook, roughly two weeks before his death; bracketed lines were crossed out)

Come then, come, you last thing I have learned,
incurable pain within the body's tissues:
as once I burned in spirit, look, I burn
in you; for a long time still the wood could resist you,
could fight against the flame as which you blazed,
but now I feed you and I burn in you.
All that's gentle turns, in the furor that's seized
my insides, into a fury of hell, not here.

Pure and aimless, free from future, I
have mounted the heaped-up pyre of suffering;
for this heart's price I know I cannot buy
anything anywhere to restock its silence.
Is that still me, burning unrecognizable there?
I cannot drag my memories back inside.
O life. Life: to be outside.
And I am in the inferno. No one knows me.

[Letting go. This isn't how sickness was
in childhood. A postponement. An excuse
to grow up. Everything cried and whispered.
Don't mix with this what earlier amazed you]

SHAWL

O Flucht aus uns und Zu-Flucht in den Shawl,
und, um die stille Mitte, das Begehren,
es möchte noch einmal und noch einmal
die unerhörte Blume wiederkehren

die sich vollzieht im schwingenden Geweb

SHAWL

Wie, für die Jungfrau, dem, der vor ihr kniet, die Namen
zustürzen unerhört: Stern, Quelle, Rose, Haus,
und wie er immer weiß, je mehr der Namen kamen,
es reicht kein Name je für ihr Bedeuten aus –

. . . so, während du sie siehst, die leichthin ausgespannte
Mitte des Kaschmirshawls, die aus dem Blumensaum
sich schwarz erneut und klärt in ihres Rahmens Kante
und einen reinen Raum schafft für den Raum . . :

erfährst du dies: daß Namen sich an ihr
endlos verschwenden: denn sie ist die Mitte.
Wie es auch sei, das Muster unsrer Schritte,
um eine solche Leere wandeln wir.

Ihr genauer Bericht über Weltrus (das ich – dem Namen nach
– seit Kindheit kenne) hat mich außerordentlich interessiert;
dieser Park voll baulicher Überraschungen, wie man sie im aus-
gehenden achtzehnten Jahrhundert so sehr liebte, als gälte es,

On Shawls and Lemons

I   (*October 1923; unfinished*)

O flight from us and flight into the shawl –
around this quiet center, the desire
to see return once more and then once more
the incredible flower consummating all
of itself within the swaying weave . . . . .

II   (*October 1923; unfinished*)

As, for the virgin, from he who kneels before her,
names rush in unheard: spring, rose, house, star . . .
and as he has always known that the more names come
not one will be enough for what she means –

. . . so, while you look at the casually outspread center
of the cashmere shawl, reborn in black
from its flowered edge, a clearing in its frame,
creating a purer space for all of space . . :

you realize: that names would be forever
wasted on it: for it is the center.
As, whatever pattern may guide our steps,
it is around a void like this we wander.

III   (*December 1923*)

. . . Yes, I know Weltrus Park [near Prague] – I've known it, at
least by name, since my childhood – so I was extraordinarily
interested to read the descriptions in your last letter: this park
full of the architectural caprices they loved so much at the end

eine solche, an einen Wohngedanken repräsentativ angeschlossene Umgebung, nicht nur zum zentralen Schloß hingebunden zu halten, sondern auch wieder diese zu steife und stramme Bindung zu lockern, durch das Nebenspiel kleiner Architekturen, die sich ihrerseits auch wieder wichtig nehmen und, jede einzelne, stark genug sind, ein paar Bosketts zu beschäftigen und ein paar Wege zu sich zu verführen. Diese Solo-Stimmen im Großen und Ganzen der orchestralen Disposition können von unbeschreiblicher Bezauberung sein, manchmal sind sie wie ein Solo der Stille, wenn man den übrigen Park in seiner vielfältigen Musik plötzlich aus dem Gefühl verliert, um auf das Abseitssein einer solchen Mühle, eines solchen Tempelchens oder einfach einer »*chaumière de plaisir*« einzugehen. – Wieviel wunderbare Übersetzungen seiner Erfahrung und Selbstkenntnis hat sich doch der menschliche Geist geschaffen –, wie diskret und geständig zugleich übertrug er sich in das Wesen einer solchen Anlage, spannte und rühmte sich in ihr auf seine Art, wie die Welt sich im Sternen-Himmel spannt und rühmt.

In Malans, bei meinem Freunde Guido Salis, hab ich viel an das Taxus-Ehepaar zu Adamocz denken müssen; denn wir beschäftigten uns viel damit, eine alte Taxus-Anlage (in dem italienisch disponierten alten Schloßgarten) im Geiste wenigstens, zu rekonstruieren. Da war, unter irgendeinem der Salis'schen Vorfahren, eine Chambre de Verdure geschaffen worden, ein kleiner hochgewachsener Saal aus sorgfältig verbundenen, einst beschnitten gewesenen Taxus-Bäumen, darin es (vermutlich) Nischen mit Statuen, Urnen und dergleichen gegeben haben mag. Nun ist dieses immergrüne Zimmer längst leer und löcherig, (unter dem Vorwand, daß es schlecht geworden sei,) ist viel von dem (als Holz) kostbaren Geäst ausgesägt worden –, und so ist das architektonisch Geschlossene dieses lebendigen Innenraums nur noch mit Hülfe der Phantasie vorstellbar; was aber noch ohne weiteres fühlbar bleibt, ist die wunderbare Berechtigung dieses dunkeln Intérieurs in seiner Funktion, einen Übergang darzustellen, zwischen der ganz in Buchs gerahmten Ordnung des Schloßgartens und, draußen, der ausgedehnten, von zerstreutem Baumbestand überwachten Wiese,

of the eighteenth century. It is as though an environment so imposingly bound up with the concept of residence had to stay closely bound to a central castle, but at the same time had to loosen this too tight bond with a panoply of other little structures, each of which takes itself seriously too and is powerful enough to dispose a few copses of its own and tempt a few paths in its direction. These solo voices amid the orchestral arrangement of the whole can be indescribably enchanting; sometimes they are like a solo of silence, when suddenly you lose your sense of the rest of the park in all its manifold music and arrive at one of these isolated mills or little temples or just a *"chaumière de plaisir."* – How many wonderful translations of its experience and self-knowledge the human spirit has managed to create for itself! how tastefully, but nevertheless revealingly, it has translated itself into the form of a landscape design like this! The human spirit displays itself and admires itself in this park the way the world displays and admires itself in the starry sky.

In Malans, at the estate of my friend Guido Salis, I have often been reminded of the husband-and-wife yew trees at your estate at Adamocz, because we were very busy reconstructing an old yew park (a château garden arranged in an Italian style), or at least reconstructing it in our imagination. One of the Salis ancestors had had a *chambre de verdure* built there: a high old hallway made of yew trees, carefully joined together long ago, in which (presumably) there must have been recesses with statues, urns, and the like. Now this evergreen chamber is long since empty and full of holes, much of the valuable (as wood goes) branches have been sawed out under the pretext that they had rotted – and so the architectonic unity of this living interior space can only be conceived with the help of the imagination. What can still be felt quite easily, though, is how wonderfully suited this interior is to its role as a passage through which you cross between the orderly château garden, framed entirely with box trees, and, outside, the expanse of fields watched over by scattered tree stock, which you can tell belongs to the château only at the exit with its two poplars. There too, by the way, to

die ihre Schloßzugehörigkeit dann erst am Ausgang durch zwei Pappeln zu erkennen gibt. Auch da gibt es dann übrigens, rechts und links von dem Taxus-Zimmer, oder besser überhalb und unterhalb seiner (da sich die ganze Anlage in Terrassen abspielt) zwei bauliche Dépendancen: die »Ruine« und die »Volière«, beide heute verfallen –, und die Wiese drüber hinaus heißt und hieß, als ob diese Ländlichkeit denn auch durch einen Namen bestätigt sein sollte (kein Mensch weiß wieso): »Das Josephle«. Draußen im »Josephle«, ein paar hundert Schritte vom Schloß, aber jenseits jener Chambre de Verdure, in der man offenbar vergaß, was man hinter sich ließ, wurde in früheren Zeiten der Tee oder sogar eine Art Pick-nick eingenommen, um dieser proponierten Landschaftlichkeit in jeder Weise recht zu geben. Man sah hin, unwillkürlich, mit dem Wunsch, unter den alten Bäumen lichte Kleider zu sehen, die Frauen und Mädchen von einst –, ebenso vergangen nun (würde ein melancholischer Dichter aus ihren Tagen versichern) wie das zitternde Spiel der Laubschatten auf ihren Sommerkleidern . . . Nein, *nicht* ebenso vergangen, behauptet unsereiner nachdenklich, nicht ebenso vergangen vielleicht, denn: was wissen wir . . .

Übrigens steckt das ganze ausgedehnte Schloß zu Malans, der sogenannte »Bothmar«, voller Ahnenbilder, und das war unsere andere Beschäftigung, in Gängen, Treppenhäusern und Zimmern auf ihre irgendwie unpräzise und doch unnachgiebige Gegenwart einzugehen (mit der sie recht haben mögen, da sie ja ihr Unerklärliches nicht wollen erklärt, sondern – wie sie es selber mußten – hingenommen haben). Diese betrachtenden Promenaden die Gänge entlang, waren sehr anregend, da mein Freund, wie kaum einer, die Geschichte seines verbreiteten Geschlechts kennt, und sie bekamen einen besonderen Reiz durch die zahlreichen Frauen- und Kinder-Bildnisse aus allen Jahrhunderten. Die Herren im Harnisch und im Staatskleid, so groß sie sich geben und so groß man sie hinnimmt, sagen ja nicht das letzte Wort –, das bleibt den Kinder- und Frauen-Bildern überlassen, die es dann, auf ihre Weise, – verschweigen.

In diesem Zusammenhange gedachte ich – fällt mir eben rechtzeitig ein – Ihre Auskunft in Anspruch zu nehmen: unter

the left and right of the yew-chamber (or, more exactly, above and below it, since the whole park is laid out in terraces), are two architectural *dépendances* – the "*Ruine*" and the "*Volière*"– both in disrepair today; and the fields outside are called, and were called, as though this piece of countryside had to be acknowledged with a name of its own as well, "the Josephle" (no one knows why). Outside in the "Josephle," a few hundred steps from the château but beyond this *chambre de verdure* where you apparently forgot what lay behind you, they used to take their tea, or even have a sort of picnic, to do justice to this landscapery that they had declared into existence. We looked out into the fields, unconsciously hoping to see bright white clothes under the old trees, the women and girls from long ago – , no less bygone now (a melancholy poet of their era would insist) than the shimmering play of the shadows through the foliage on their summer dresses. . . . No, *not* as bygone, a poet of our era would thoughtfully maintain, not as bygone perhaps, for, after all, what do we know. . . .

In any case, the whole sprawl of the Malans château, the so-called "Bothmar," is full of ancestral portraits. That was our other occupation here: entering, in the passageways, the stair-wells, the rooms, into these portraits' somehow imprecise but still unyielding presence (and in this they may well be right, since what they want is for their inexplicabilities not to be explained but rather to be – as they must be – taken in). These promenades along the passageways inspecting the portraits were very stimulating, since my friend knows the history of his far-flung line like almost no one else; they became even more attractive thanks to the numerous portraits of women and children from every century. The lords, in their armor and formal attire, however grand they give themselves out to be or are taken to be, do not have the last word, not at all – that is left to the pictures of the children and the women, who then, in their way . . . keep silent.

In this context, I thought – the idea struck me right away – of requesting your kind assistance. We noticed that in several of the most impressive portraits of women from the seven-

den stattlichsten Frauen-Porträts des siebzehnten und acht-
zehnten Jahrhunderts fielen mehrere uns dadurch auf, daß die
Dargestellte in ihren gelassen zur Schau gehaltenen Händen,
unaufdringlich und doch mit einer gewissen, dem Symbol zu-
zuschreibenden Betonung, immer wieder den gleichen Gegen-
stand hielt: eine Citrone. Salis war der Meinung, es sei mit diesem
stereotypen (übrigens meistens recht stark und ausdrücklich
gemalten) Attribut ausgesprochen, daß seine Trägerin zur Zeit,
als man sie so, mit dem Anschein ihres blühenden oder beträcht-
lichen Lebens wiedergab, schon verstorben gewesen sei; er war
indessen dieser Auslegung nicht ganz sicher, die Frage blieb
offen. Ich freute mich darauf, sie gelegentlich an Sie weiter-
zugeben; vielleicht haben Sie im eigenen Hause ähnliche
Darstellungen oder erinnern, solche gesehen, von solchen gehört
zu haben. Ist das wirklich die Bedeutung der mitgegebenen
Citrone, so bleibt es ja immer noch unerklärt, wie diese Frucht
zu dieser bildlichen Anwendung kam. Ich wüßte nicht, daß sie
in irgendwelchen Toten-Kulten eine Rolle gespielt haben sollte;
ist es diese Verbindung von letzter Bitterkeit und Reife, die sie
zum Zeichen des Verstorbenseins machen konnte –, das käme
mir schon fast zu abgeleitet und ausgeklügelt vor. (Ihr Duft
übrigens, der Duft dieser Frucht, hat für mich eine unbeschreib-
liche Eindringlichkeit; ich habe immer, den Winter über, wo
den Sinnen so viel Einflüsse von außenher abgehen, eine Glas-
schale mit Citronen im Arbeitszimmer. Ihre Bitterkeit, so
zusammenziehend sie im Geschmack sich geltend macht, als
Duft eingeatmet, gibt sie mir eine Sensation von reiner Weite
und Offenheit –; wie oft habe ichs bedauert, daß wir allen der-
artigen Erfahrungen gegenüber so endgültig verstummt, so
sprachlos bleiben. Wie *erleb* ich ihn, diesen Citronengeruch,
weiß Gott, was ich ihm zu Zeiten verdanke . . . , und wenn ich
wirklich, wörtlich wiederholen soll, *was* er mir in die Sinne dik-
tiert: Fiasko!)

Wie eingeschränkt ist doch immerfort das Gebiet unseres
Beredtseins; in Bern kürzlich (ich ging dorthin von Malans
über Zürich) überlegt ichs wieder. Dort ist jedesmal das »His-
torische Museum« das große Ereignis für mich durch seine

teenth and eighteenth centuries, the woman's hand would calmly display the same object over and over again: a lemon. Not insistently, but still with a certain emphasis, to be attributed to the object's symbolic nature. Salis thought that this formulaic attribute (which was, by the way, usually painted with great force and expression) meant that its bearer, when painted like this with all the appearance of blossoming or fulsome life, had already died. He was, however, not entirely sure of this interpretation; it remained an open question. I looked forward to passing it on to you when the opportunity arose; you may perhaps have, in your own house, similar images, or may recall having seen some, or heard of some. Even if that really is what a lemon in the person's hand signifies, it remains a mystery to me how it came to acquire this particular pictorial function. Lemons have no role in any cult of the dead that I know of; could it be the connection between a final bitterness and maturity that makes the lemon a sign of having died? That strikes me as too far-fetched, too clever an explanation. (Their scent, by the way, the smell of this fruit, makes an indescribably powerful impression on me: all winter, when so many of the impressions that reach our senses from without have departed, I have always kept a glass bowl of lemons in the room where I work. Their bitterness, however much it makes your mouth pucker up when you taste them, gives me, when I breathe it in as a smell, a sensation of pure breadth and openness. I have often regretted that we so decisively fall silent when faced with any experience like that; we remain so speechless. How I *experienced* it at the time, this odor of lemons! God knows how much I owe to it . . . and then, when I try to truly, accurately repeat *what* it dictated to my senses: disaster!)

How limited it always is, though, the domain of our eloquence. That thought came to me again in Bern recently (I traveled there from Malans via Zurich). Every time I go there the great thing for me is the Historical Museum, because of its incredibly splendid tapestries, Burgundian treasures seized in the fifteenth-century Swiss victory over Charles the Bold. This magnificent collection has recently been enlarged in the other

unerhört herrlichen Wand-Teppiche, die die Schweizer des fünf-
zehnten Jahrhunderts aus dem Burgunder-Schatz Karls des
Kühnen sich erobert hatten. Diese prächtigen Sammlungen
sind seit kurzem nach anderen Seiten hin bereichert durch den
Nachlaß eines Sammlers von Orientalien; Miniaturen, Waffen,
Kacheln, Bronzen von ungleichem Wert; diesmal aber kam ich
auf eine besondere Entdeckung: Shawls: persische und tur-
kestanische Kaschmir-Shawls, wie sie auf den sanft abfallenden
Schultern unserer Ur-Großmütter zu rührender Geltung kamen;

Shawls mit runder oder quadratischer oder sternig ausgesparter
Mitte, mit schwarzem, grünem oder elfenbein-weißem Grund,
jeder eine Welt für sich, ja wahrhaftig, jeder ein ganzes Glück,
eine ganze Seligkeit und vielleicht ein ganzer Verzicht, – jeder
alles dies, voll von menschlichem Einschlag, jeder ein Garten,
in dem der ganze Himmel dieses Gartens miterzählt, mitent-
halten war, wie im Citronen-Duft wahrscheinlich der ganze
Raum, die ganze Umwelt sich mitteilt, die die glückliche Frucht
in ihr Wachstum Tag und Nacht einbezog. Wie vor Jahren in
Paris die Spitzen, so begriff ich plötzlich, vor diesen ausgebrei-
teten und abgewandelten Geweben, das Wesen des Shawls!
Aber es *sagen?* Wieder ein Fiasko. Nur *so* vielleicht, nur in den
Verwandlungen, die ein greifliches langsames Hand-Werk er -
laubt, ergeben sich vollzählige, verschwiegene Äquivalente des
Lebens, zu denen die Sprache immer nur umschreibend gelangt,
es sei denn es gelänge ihr ab und zu, im magischen Anruf zu
erreichen, daß irgendein geheimeres Gesicht des Daseins uns,
im Raume eines Gedichts, zugekehrt bleibt.

[SHAWL]

Wie Seligkeit in diesem sich verbirgt,
so eingewirkt, daß nichts mehr sie zerstöre,
wie bloßes Spiel vollkommener Akteure
so ungebraucht ins Dauern eingewirkt.

So eingewirkt in schmiegende Figur
ins leichte Wesen dieser Ziegenwolle,

direction with the gift of a collector of Eastern art: miniatures, weapons, tiles, bronzes, some more valuable, some less; but this time I made a special discovery: shawls: Persian and Turkic cashmere shawls like the ones that showed off the gently sloping shoulders of our great-great-grandmothers to their best advantage; shawls with a round or square or star-shaped space in the center, with a black or green or ivory-white background, each one a world in itself, truly, each one a whole happiness, a whole bliss, perhaps a whole renunciation, – all of this in each and every one, full of humanity, every one of them a garden in which all of the heavens above the garden are contained, are told; just as the scent of the lemons communicates along with it the whole sky, the whole environment that included this happy fruit, day and night, as it grew. Just like the lace, years ago in Paris – I suddenly understood, in front of this outspread and various weaving, the essence of the shawl! But to say it? Again a disaster. Maybe *this* is the only way – maybe only in the metamorphosis permitted by slow and tangible handwork can reticent but complete equivalents of life come into being, the life that language can always only describe, even if language does manage, now and then, in a magical summons, to keep one or another of the secret faces of existence turned to us, in the space of a poem.

IV   (*July 1924; unfinished*)

As bliss takes shelter here, so worked in
that nothing more will ever destroy it;
as onstage any accomplished actors
can inexhaustibly work in us;

so worked in, into the nestling shapes,
in the easy manner of the wool

ganz pures Glück, unbrauchbar von Natur
rein aufgegeben an das wundervolle

Geweb in das das Leben überging.
O wieviel Regung rettet sich ins reine
Bestehn und Überstehn von einem Ding.

is joy: unusable by nature,
abandoned, pure and wonderful,

to the weave that life passes over into.
O how our efforts escape into
a thing's existence, pure persistence. . . .

Es ist ganz stille. Aufrecht steht der Duft
vergangner Farben in den welken Wegen.
Die Himmel halten einen langen Regen
die Blätter gehn auf Stufen durch die Luft

There is total silence. Upright in overgrown
paths stands the scent of bygone color.
The sky holds back a long hard rain
The leaves climb stairways through the air

I

Die Brunnen in der *Certosa*. In einem, tiefen sieht man das
Lichte des Himmels, fast ohne sein Blau; das Querholz, an dem
die Brunnenrolle hängt, scheint silbern unten; seltsam ist Grün,
wenn es unten erscheint. Und die Gesichter. Nach den Gesetzen
der pompejanischen Farbigkeit. Clara sagt: so ist es im Leben:
da können wir auch nichts sehen, ohne selbst mit hinein-
zukommen. – Man zeigt uns die kleinen Gefängnis-Zellen, die
für die Strafkompagnie seinerzeit in Gebrauch waren. Neben
dem Holzlager bleibt nur ein schmaler Raum, hinter dem sich
gleich die Türe schließt, ein Gitter zuerst, darauf eine dicke
Eichentür mit kleinem Schubfenster. Wenn man sich für einen
Moment drinnen hat einschließen lassen, kommt man wie
nach langer Zeit heraus, als ob drinnen andere Minuten wären;
ebenso empfand man Licht und Sonne nach dem Aufstieg von
der unteren Cisterne her. –

II

Im Museum von Neapel standen wir lange vor dem Orpheus-
Relief diesmal; wir fragten uns, ob nicht hier doch wieder das
Stoffliche einen Streich spiele? Wir sahen antike Gläser mit den
herrlichen ungleichmäßigen Farben und den Fruchtformen.
Wir blieben sehr lange vor den pompejanischen Bildern; erst,
neulich, vor dem, welches Clara wiedergefunden hatte; jenem
Jüngling, wie er von rechts unten her, nach dem Meer hinauf-
steigt, vor dessen Weite, wie ein Eingang, zwei wartende helle
Frauengestalten über die Felsenufer hinausragen. Dann, an
diesem Tage, vor den Tafeln auf dem Drehpult: der Blumen-
pflückenden, Abgewendeten, Weißen, die zurücklangend in
den malachitgrünen Wachsgrund hineinschreitet. Der anderen
Weißen, die in etwas mehr als Profil ihr gesenktes Gesicht zeigt,
nachdenklich, während ihre Hände, ein wenig in den blauen

From the Notebooks

I (*Naples, January 1907*)

The wells in the Certosa di San Martino. In one deep well you
see the light of the sky almost without its blue; down there the
wooden crossbar, which the well wheel hangs from, shines sil-
ver; how strange the green looks when it appears down there.
And the faces. They follow the laws of Pompeiian coloration.
Clara says: That's how it is in life too: we can't see anything unless
we ourselves enter into it. – They show us the little prison cells,
which were used in their day for a penal company. Beside the
woodshed all that's left is a narrow space and right behind
it the door closes, first bars and then a thick oak door with a
little sliding window. If you let yourself be shut in there for a
moment, you come out as though after a long time, as though
there were different minutes inside; that is exactly how you per-
ceived the light and the sun after climbing back up from the
lower cisterns. –

II

In the Naples museum, we stood for a long while in front of
the relief of Orpheus this time; we asked ourselves if the mate-
rial world wasn't perhaps up to its old tricks again? We saw
antique glasses with their magnificent irregular colors and fruit-
shapes. We stayed a very long time in front of the Pompeiian
pictures: first, the other day, in front of the one that Clara
remembered from before – the young man climbing up from
the bottom right, toward the ocean, in front of whose breadth,
like an entrance, two bright waiting female figures jut out from
the rocky shore. Then, this time, in front of the tablets on the
rotating display case: the flower picker, facing away, white, reach-
ing back into the malachite-green wax background as she
strides into it. The other white figure, who shows her down-
turned face in a bit more than profile, thoughtfully, while her

Grund vorragend, einen Pfeil an den noch ungespannten Bogen legen. Da ist wieder eine von den leisen, gleichsam ausgesparten Handlungen, die mit nichts verratender vielsagender Feierlichkeit vor sich gehen gleich jenen in den Teppichen der Dame à la Licorne unvergleichlich dargestellten. Wie es die Farben sind, so ist hier auch, mit ihnen und durch sie, der Ausdruck auf Nuancen gestellt, auf das Leise, das Langsame und die Gewalt, die von ihm ausgeht.

III

Das Meer unter nahem grauem Himmel in drei Streifen herbewegt; der fernste schwarz und schwer; der mittlere in beständiger Erhebung, dunkelflaschengrün; der nahe ebene: sich in Schichten übereinanderschiebender kalkweißer Schaum. Wo der zweite Streifen in den nächsten hineinfällt entsteht in jeder Welle ein lichtgrüner unbeschreiblich heller durchscheinender Sturz, durch den man das Innere der Woge sieht, eine Sekunde lang, ehe sie im Schaum ihres eigenen Niederfalls verloren geht.

IV

Sprich von den Weinbergen zur Zeit, da an einem windigen Tag (der früh mit Sonne begann, dann aber in einem dünnen Grau sich auflöste) die ersten Arbeiten an ihnen beginnen. Da sind sie eine Harmonie in Grau und Gold, jenem Grau und jenem Gold von Hölzern, das man aus gewissen Intarsien kennt. Das Grau ist in mehreren Arten vertreten, in vielen Abstufungen und von jeder sind nur Streifen da, Ausschnitte, Stücke, die ganz dicht an andere Streifen anschließen. Und auch die Leute, die da zwischen den grauen Stützen und den holzgoldenen Ranken ihre Arbeit verrichten, vor dem zusammengesetzten Hintergrund der Terrassenmauern, sind wie aus grauen Hölzern gefügt und in das Ganze hineingelegt, so daß man sie erst allmählich unterscheidet. Dann und wann schiebt ein Feigenbaum sein reiches steigendes Ornament dazwischen,

hands, reaching forward a little into the blue background, place an arrow into the still-unbent bow. Here again is one of those quiet actions, so quiet it is all but left totally blank, that happens of itself with a festiveness that says much but betrays nothing, like the actions incomparably presented in the Lady and the Unicorn tapestries. As with those colors, here too, with them and through them, the emphasis is placed on the nuances, on stillness, on slowness and the violence that streams out from it.

III (*Capri, January–February 1907*)

The ocean, under a close gray sky, comes toward us in three bands: the distant one black and heavy; the middle one constantly rising and churning, dark bottle-green; the near one smooth: one layer of chalk-white foampushing across the next. Where the second band falls down into the third, every swell becomes a light-green, indescribably bright, translucent tumble, through which you can see the inside of the wave, for a second, before it is lost in the foam of its own fall.

IV

Describe the vineyards at the moment when, on a windy day (it began with early sunshine, but then disintegrated into a thin gray), the first work in them begins. They are a harmony in gray and gold, the same gray and the same gold as the wood we know from certain intarsia. The gray is represented by several types, in many gradations, and there are only bands of each kind, cutouts, pieces, joined tight to the other strips. The people, too, performing their labors there between the gray supports and the wood-gold shoots, in front of the assembled background of terrace walls, the people too are as if put together out of gray pieces of wood, so that you can only gradually distinguish them. Here and there a fig tree pushes its rich, ascending ornamentation between them, while farther up an olive tree, its leaves turned by the wind, extends the tonal scale into a

während weiter oben eine Olive mit den windgewendeten Blät-
tern um ein sonst noch nirgends gebrauchtes bewegteres Grau
die Gamme vergrößert, und ein kleiner Vogel zwischen alledem
einen Flecken seltenes kostbares Rot anbringt, einen winzigen
Flecken, dessen rascher Kontrast aber genügt das Auge für die
tausend Abwandlungen des Graus noch schauender zu machen.

(Straße nach der piccola Marina)

[ENTWÜRFE]

– als wäre meine schwere
Kindheit ganz aus Silber

Uns verwirrt es, die wir seiend heißen
immer so zu leben: nur von Bildern;
und wir möchten manchesmal mit wildern
Griffen Wirklichkeiten in uns reißen
Stücke, Abzufühlendes, ein Sein

HERBST-ABEND

Wind aus dem Mond,
plötzlich ergriffene Bäume
und ein tastend fallendes Blatt.
Durch die Zwischenräume
der schwachen Laternen
drängt die schwarze Landschaft der Fernen
in die unentschlossene Stadt.

more mobile gray that has never been used anywhere before, and a little bird brings its patch of rare, precious red into all that, a tiny dot whose quick contrast is enough to awaken the eye even more to the thousand vicissitudes of gray.

(*Road to Marina Piccola*)

V (*Paris, Fall 1907*)

– as though all my hard childhood
were made of silver. . . .

It confuses us, we for whom being means
to live only, always, from images;
sometimes we want to grab wildly
at realities, draw them inside us –
pieces, things we can feel with our hands, that which *is*

AUTUMN EVENING

Wind from the moon,
trees suddenly seized,
a tentative falling leaf.
The black landscape of afar
pushes through the space
between weak lanterns
into an undecided city.

Alle Fahnen sind höher hinaufgehalten

Und im Herbst der welkenden Façaden
Grau begreifen bis heran ans Rot,
mit dem vielen Leben überladen
das gedrängt aus allen Dingen droht.

Wenn das Gefühl einer der fernen Städte
sich plötzlich an dich klammert, an dir hält,
als ob es nirgends eine Stelle hätte
als nur in dir: als wärest du die Welt.

All of the flags are held up higher......

And in autumn to understand the gray
of the fading façades, right up to the red,
ornately overloaded with all
that tight-pressed life that threatens from things.

When the feeling of one of the distant cities
suddenly grips you, holds you tight,
as though there were no other place for it
except in you: as though you were the world.

Sehnsucht

Voilà la nuit t'ouvrant ses bras d'espace
Vas-y te blottir comme un jeune amant,
ferme les yeux à ce moindre vent
et tu auras sa face sur ta face

Ich segne dich mit meinen Überflüssen,
die sich in meinen Liedern nicht verbrauchen.
Ich werde leise in dein Schlafen tauchen
und dir von innen deine Lider küssen ...

Night Songs

I I (*1911, age thirty-five*)

Look – night is opening her arms of sky to you
Cuddle up to her like a young man in love,
then shut your eyes at the slightest breeze
and you will feel her face on your face

II (*1900, age twenty-four*)

With all my abundances I bless you;
in all my songs they never run dry.
I sink softly into your sleep and kiss you
on the eyelids from inside . . .

Schön hab ichs aufgefaßt, wie mirs noch nie sich darstellte: dieses immer weiter Hineinverlegtsein des entstehenden Geschöpfs aus der Welt in die Innen-Welt. Daher die reizende Lage des Vogels auf diesem Wege nach Innen; sein Nest ist ja fast ein von der Natur ihm bewilligter äußerer Mutterleib, den er nur ausstattet und zudeckt, statt ihn ganz zu enthalten. So ist er dasjenige von den Tieren, das zur Außenwelt eine ganz besondere Gefühlsvertraulichkeit hat, als wüßte er sich mit ihr im innigsten Geheimnis. Darum singt er in ihr, als sänge er in seinem Innern, darum fassen wir einen Vogellaut so leicht ins Innere auf, es scheint uns, als übersetzten wir ihn, ohne Rest, in unser Gefühl, ja er kann uns, für einen Augenblick, die ganze Welt zum Innenraum machen, weil wir fühlen, daß der Vogel nicht unterscheidet zwischen seinem Herzen und dem ihren. –

Note on Birds

I've figured it out, something that was never clear to me before
– how all of creation transposes itself out of the world deeper
and deeper into our inner world, and why birds cast such a spell
on this path into us. The bird's nest is, in effect, an outer womb
given by nature; the bird only furnishes it and covers it rather
than containing the whole thing inside itself. As a result, birds
are the animals whose feelings have a very special, intimate
familiarity with the outer world; they know that they share
with nature their innermost mystery. That is why the bird sings
its songs into the world as though it were singing into its inner
self, that's why we take a birdsong into our own inner selves so
easily, it seems to us that we translate it fully, with no remain-
der, into our feelings; a birdsong can even, for a moment, make
the whole world into a sky within us, because we feel that the
bird does not distinguish between its heart and the world's.

VORFRÜHLING

Härte schwand. Auf einmal legt sich Schonung
an der Wiesen aufgedecktes Grau.
Kleine Wasser ändern die Betonung.
Zärtlichkeiten, ungenau,

greifen nach der Erde aus dem Raum.
Wege gehen weit ins Land und zeigens.
Unvermutet siehst du seines Steigens
Ausdruck in dem leeren Baum.

LIED FÜR HELENE

Wir alle brauchen solchen warmen Regen
wie er in diesen Nächten flutend fiel, –
so muß der Himmel seine Hände legen
in unsrer Seelen sanftes Saitenspiel
damit ein Frühling drin beginnt.
Dann laß den Wind
allein mit Deinem Liede,
und sei nicht bang, daß er es Dir entreißt:
Aus Deiner ersten Furcht kommt lauter Friede
wenn Du Dein Lied auf Flügeln weißt.

Spring Songs

I Early Spring (*1924, age forty-eight*)

Hardness has vanished. Suddenly solace
descends on the uncovered gray of the meadows.
Small streams change the emphasis.
Down, imprecisely, come caresses

towards the earth from the sky.
Paths go deep into the land and show it.
You unexpectedly see it grow. It
expresses itself in an empty tree.

II Song for Helene (*1899, age twenty-three*)

We all need warm rains like the one that's been
flooding down the past few nights, –
this must be how heaven lays its hands
on the soft stringed instruments of our souls
so that, within them, spring can begin.
Then leave the wind
alone, with your song,
don't be scared that the wind will tear it from you:
out of your first fear comes nothing but peace
when you see how your song has taken wing.

Nicht daß uns, da wir (plötzlich) erwachsen sind
und plötzlich mit-schuldig an unvor-
denklicher Schuld der Erwachsenen; Mitwisser plötzlich
aller Gewissen –, nicht daß uns dann ein Häscher errät
und handfest hinüber zerrt und zurück
ins vergangne Gefängnis, wo von der Zeit nur
Abwässer sind, die weggeschüttete Zukunft,
draus eine Welle manchmal mit fast ihm
entgangener Hand der Gefangene aufhebt, sie über
      den kahlge-
schorenen Kopf hinschüttend wie irgendein Kommen,

– – – – – – – – – – – – – – – – – – – –

das nicht [ist unser Ärgstes,]; sondern die Kerker von früh an
die sich aus unserem Atem bilden, aus einer zu zeitig
verstandenen Hoffnung, aus selber
unserem Schicksal. Aus der noch eben
rein durchdringlichen offenen Luft, aus jedem Geschauten.

Wie so mag ein Mädchen auf einmal durch Gitter
seiner Noch-Kindheit den Liebbaren sehn, getrennter
als in Legende. Ihm gegenüber
aufschaun, um ins Vorfrauliche traurig
abzugleiten von ihm.
Oder Getrennten sind mehr. Jahrzehnt und Jahrtausend
von Gesicht zu Gesicht. Und zwischen Erkannten
steht vielleicht im Kerker der Kindheit das besser,
das unendlich berechtigte Herz.

(unfinished; bracketed phrases crossed out by Rilke)

It's not that now that we're (suddenly) grown up
and suddenly complicit with the im-
memorial guilt of adults; accessory suddenly
to all conscience – , it's not that then the pursuer reaches
us, drags us violently back over there
into bygone prisons, where all that's left
of time is sewage, the dumped-out future,
and from it the prisoner sometimes with a hand
that has almost escaped him lifts up a wave and pours it out
    over the sha-
ven head like some advent,

–––––––––––––––––––

[*that's* not the worst thing for us,] it's not *that*; rather
    the dungeons from early on
that are formed from our breath, from long-ago-
understood hopes, from our very
fate. From the air even now
purely penetrable and open, from everything we see.

So might a girl, all at once, through the bars
of her still-just-a-childhood, see her future beloved, separated
from her as in legends. Facing him she might
look up, only to glide off into pre-womanhood, sadly,
away from him.
Or the separations are more. Decade, millennium
from face to face. And between them as they recognize
    each other
stands perhaps in the dungeon of childhood the better,
the endlessly rightful heart.

[Mann, sei wie ein Engel,
wenn die Begegnung geschieht und es geht noch das Mädchen
eingelassen einher im Gleichnis der Kindheit.
[Nicht ein Begehrender, welcher bestünde]
Sei wie ein Engel. Laß sie nicht rückwärts. Weiter
gieb ihr die Freiheit. Über das bloße
Lieben gieb ihr die Gnade der Liebe. Bewußtsein
gieb ihr der Ströme. Kühnheit der Himmel
stürze um sie. Durch den empfundenen Herzraum
wirf ihr die Vögel]
[Kerker unsägliche, unvermutete Kerker]

[Man, be like an angel
when the encounter takes place and the girl
goes down into it in a parable of childhood.
[Not someone desiring, who would consist]
Be like an angel. Don't leave her behind. More,
give her freedom. Above and beyond mere
loving, give her the grace of love. Give her consciousness
of rivers. The boldness of heaven,
cast it around her. Throw birds
at her through the heart's felt sky.]
[Dungeons unspeakable, unsuspected dungeons]

Ich erfand mir eine neue Zärtlichkeit: Eine Rose leise auf das geschlossene Auge zu legen, bis sie mit ihrer Kühle kaum mehr fühlbar ist und nur die Sanftmut ihres Blattes noch über dem Lid ruht, wie [ein Stück] Schlaf vor Sonnenaufgang.

FRAGMENT: Als der Tod mit dem Morgen kam, war ihr vieles Leben ganz in ihr Gesicht eingetreten. Von dort riß es der Tod, und er hat ihren mädchenkühlen Leib nicht angerührt. Aber rasch sprang sein kurzer Griff aus ihrem gedrängten Gesicht zurück, wie aus weichem Ton, und ließ alle Züge weit ausgezogen, lang und scharf zurück. Georg konnte dieses spitze Kinn und diese dünne Nase, auf deren Kante der Schatten hart abgegrenzt war, nicht sehen. Er ging hinaus, brach mit bösem Blick zwei harte herbstliche Knospen von roten Rosen, die frostig und beschlagen in der Herbstluft standen, ging mit den beiden sehr schweren Blüten im Garten umher und kam von selbst wieder in das Zimmer zu seiner mädchenhaften Toten. Es quälte ihn, daß der letzte Blick noch immer dunkel in ihren offenen Augen stand. Er drückte ihre breiten weißen Lider zu, indem er sie zitternd unter der Stirn hervorzog, und legte auf jedes Lid eine harte Rose, schwer. Dann erst konnte er das Angesicht der Gestorbenen ruhig betrachten. Und je länger er es ansah, desto mehr empfand er, daß noch eine Welle Leben an den Rand ihrer Züge herangespült war, die sich langsam wieder nach innen zurückzog. Er erinnerte sich sogar, dieses Leben, wie es jetzt auf der Stirne und um ihren überlittenen Mund lag, in sehr schönen Stunden bei ihr begrüßt zu haben, und er wußte, daß dies ihr heiligstes Leben sei, dessen Vertrauter er kaum geworden war, von dem er nur wie aus Gerüchten und Liedern wußte. – Sie war gestorben. Der Tod hatte dieses Leben nicht aus ihr geholt. Er hatte sich täuschen lassen von dem vielen Alltag in ihrem gelösten Gesichte; den hatte er ihr fortgerissen zugleich mit dem sanften Umriß ihres Profils. Aber das andere Leben war noch in ihr, vor einer Weile war es bis an den

When Death Came with the Morning
from Rilke's diary

. . . I've discovered a new caress: to lay a rose lightly across your closed eyes until you can hardly feel its coolness any more and only the gentleness of its petals still stirs on your eyelids, like a short sleep before sunrise.

FRAGMENT: When death came, with the morning, all of her life had risen into her face and death took it from there. He did not touch her cold girl's body. But then his brief grip sprang back from her shoved-in face and left all her features stretched out, long and sharp. Georg could not look at this sharp chin, this thin nose whose line marked the hard edge of shadow. He went outside and, with an angry look, broke off two hard small autumn red roses that stood frosty and misted-up in the autumn air. He walked around the garden with the two very heavy blossoms and his steps automatically brought him back into the room with his girlish corpse. It tormented him to see her last gaze even now darkly in her open eyes. He pressed her two broad white eyelids closed, by tremblingly pulling them out from under her brow, and on each lid he heavily laid a hard rose. Only then could he observe the face of the deceased in peace. And the longer he looked at it, the more he felt that a wave of life was still swirling right up to the edge of her features, and that it was slowly ebbing away, back inside. He remembered, in fact, how in certain deeply beautiful hours he had greeted this life that now lay on her brow and around this mouth that had suffered too much. And he knew that this was her holiest life, with which he was hardly familiar; which he knew about only as though from rumors or songs.

She was dead. But death had not gathered this life out of her. He had let himself be deceived by all the day-to-day existence in her relaxed face; that is what he took from her, along with the soft outline of her profile. The other life, though, was still inside her; it had flooded up to the edge of her disfigured mouth for a while and now it slowly retreated, flowed back

Rand des entstellten Mundes herangeflutet und jetzt trat es langsam zurück, floß lautlos nach innen und sammelte sich irgendwo über ihrem zersprungenen Herzen. Und Georg hatte eine unendliche Sehnsucht, dieses Leben, welches dem Tod entgangen war, zu besitzen. Er war ja der einzige, der es empfangen durfte, der Erbe ihrer Blumen und Bücher und ihrer sanften Gewänder, die noch nach der Sonne des letzten Sommers dufteten und nach ihrem leichtbewegten Leibe, – er allein konnte auch der Empfänger dieses Lebens sein, das bald nichtmehr erreichbar war für sein trauriges Auge. Er wußte nicht, wie er diese Wärme, die so unerbittlich aus den Wangen sich zurückzog, festhalten, wie er sie fassen, womit er sie nehmen sollte. Er suchte die Hand der Toten, die leer und offen, wie die Schale einer entkernten Frucht, auf der Decke lag. Die Kälte dieser Hand war gleichmäßig und still, und sie gab bereits völlig das Gefühl eines Dinges, welches eine Nacht lang im Tau gelegen hat, um dann rasch im starken Frühwind kalt und trocken zu werden. Da rührte sich plötzlich ein Schatten im Gesichte der Toten. Gespannt sah Georg hin; lange blieb alles still, dann zuckte die linke Rose. Und Georg sah: sie war viel größer geworden. Die Spitze, in der die vielen Blätter sich aneinanderfügten, war breiter geworden, und auch der Kelch unten war wie von einem Atemholen gehoben. Und es wuchs auch die Rose über dem rechten Auge. Und während das spitze Gesicht sich an den Tod gewöhnte, ruhten die Rosen immer voller und wärmer über den vergangenen Augen. – Und als es Abend geworden war nach diesem lautlosen Tage, trug Georg zwei große rote Rosen in der zitternden Hand ans Fenster. Wie in zwei Kelchen, die vor Schwere schwankten, trug er ihr Leben, den Überfluß ihres Lebens, den auch er nie empfangen hatte.

inside her without a sound and collected somewhere in her burst heart. Georg had an infinite desire to possess this life that had escaped from death. He, he was the only one who was permitted to receive it, the legacy of her flowers and books and her soft garments that still smelled of last summer's sun and her body that moved so lightly – and only he was able to receive it too, this life which his sad eyes would soon no longer be able to reach. He didn't know how to hold onto this warmth, so inexorably withdrawing from her cheeks, how to grasp it, what he could catch it with. He sought the dead girl's hand, lying empty and open on the covers like the cup of a pitted plum. The hand's coldness was quiet and regular; it already gave off the feeling of a thing that had lain all night in the dew, only to become cold and dry in a sharp early-morning wind. Then suddenly a shadow moved on the dead girl's face. Georg eagerly looked up; for a long time all was still; then the left rose trembled. And Georg saw: it had grown much bigger. The points where all the petals fit together had spread out and the calyx underneath was as if lifted up by someone's breath. And the rose on her right eye was growing bigger too. And as her sharp pointed face grew accustomed to death the roses rested, more and more full, warmer and warmer, on her departed eyes.

– And as this day without a sound turned to evening, Georg carried two large red roses in his trembling hand to the window. As though in two chalices, swaying with heaviness, he carried her life, the overflowing abundance of her life, which even he had never received.

Hebend die Blicke vom Buch, von den nahen zählbaren
      Zeilen,
in die vollendete Nacht hinaus:
o wie sich sternegemäß die gedrängten Gefühle verteilen,
so als bände man auf
einen Bauernstrauß:

Jugend der leichten und neigendes Schwanken der schweren
und der zärtlichen zögernder Bug –.
Überall Lust zu Bezug und nirgends Begehren;
Welt zu viel und Erde genug.

Looking up from the book, from the near and countable lines
out into the culminant night:
O how, like stars, the feelings crushed tight
spread out, like when you untie
a country bouquet:

Youth of the light ones and inclined sway of the heavy ones,
tender ones' hesitant prow – .
Everywhere wanting connection and nowhere desire;
too much world and earth enough.

Träume

[Bruchstück]

Der Verstorbene war ein außerordentlich großer, langer, hagerer Mann. Es gehörte nicht viel dazu, um einzusehn, daß er an gewisse harte und steile Pferde erinnerte, von denen jeder, der wenig mit Pferden zu tun hat, fürchtet, daß sie eines Tages durchgehen könnten. In Wirklichkeit tun sie es nie; aber es ist nicht unbegreiflich, daß die Leute ihnen mißtrauen. Denn in der Haltung ihres Kopfes ist eine Heftigkeit ausgesprochen, die umsomehr beunruhigt, als sie sich nicht in Bewegungen offenbart, sondern in einem zuständlichen Stillehalten, das aber, so meint man, mit etwas Heftigem begonnen haben muß und nicht anders als gewaltsam enden kann. Dieses Gefühl wird eigentümlich unterstützt durch den Blick dieser Tiere, der klagend ist, sobald man ihm zufällig begegnet. Sieht man aber in ihre Augen hinein, so sind sie aufgeregt und aufgerissen wie die offenen Augen in einem Bilde das man umdreht.

Dream

(*Fragment*)

The dead man was extraordinarily big, tall, gaunt. It didn't take much to realize that he was like those tough, stubborn horses that anyone who doesn't have much to do with horses is afraid will bolt. In fact they don't bolt, but it's easy to understand why people don't trust them: the way they hold their head expresses a certain ferocity that makes people all the more anxious because the ferocity doesn't reveal itself in movement, only in a steady holding still, which must nevertheless have begun with something ferocious, you think, so it can only end in violence. This feeling is oddly reinforced by the mournful glance of these animals whenever it happens to meet your own. But when you look deeper into their eyes you find them wide open and excited like the open eyes in a painting you've turned upside down.

Der Ursprung der Chimäre

Der Engel jüngster, als sein übersüßer
mündiger Samen stand bis an den Rand,
kam zu den offenen Heiligen ins Land.
Doch voller Mißtraun schlossen sich die Büßer
und hatten nicht den Liebenden erkannt.

Die Tiere aber waren außer sich.
Da riß der Engel seine Lust nach innen
und ging die ganze Nacht, ging und verglich
sein Auge mit dem Aug der Tigerinnen.

Bis schließlich eine büßende Hetäre
am Eingang einer Königsgruft
ihn anschrie, ob die Nacht denn ewig währe.
Da wollte er, daß diese da gebäre
(es lag ein Wesen in der Luft),
und führte sie zu Männern an der Fähre
und gab ihr wieder ihren Duft.

The Origin of the Chimera

The youngest angel, his ready too-sweet
mouth-seed filling him right to the limit,
he came to the open saints in the land.
But full of mistrust, the penitents shut
him out; they would not know the lover.

The animals, though, were beside themselves.
So he reined his lust in, dragged it inside,
and walked all night long – walked and measured
his eye against the tigresses.'

Until at last a hetæra, penitent
at the door to the crypt of the king,
cried out to him: Will this night last forever?
So then he wanted her there to bear
(there was a creature in the air)
and led her to the ferrymen
and gave her back her scent again.

Aus dem Traum-Buch
Der siebente, elfte und sechsundzwanzigste Traum

Der siebente Traum

Ich suchte das junge Mädchen. Ich fand sie in einem schmalen langen Zimmer, in dem es eben Morgen wurde. Sie saß auf einem Stuhl und lächelte kaum merklich. Neben ihr, nicht weiter als einen Schritt von ihr entfernt, stand ein zweiter Stuhl, auf dem ein junger Mensch, steif angelehnt, saß. Es schien, als hätten die beiden so die Nacht verbracht.

Das junge Mädchen rührte sich und reichte mir die Hand, indem sie sie mir hoch entgegenhob. Diese Hand war warm und irgendwie abgehärtet anzufühlen, als hielte man ein kleines Tier, das im Freien lebt und für sich selber sorgen muß.

Und nun rührte sich auch der junge Mensch. Er war sichtlich bemüht, aufzuwachen; sein Gesicht verzog sich auf eine unangenehme und ungeduldige Art. Das junge Mädchen hatte sich ein wenig zur Seite gewandt und sah ihm zu. Sein Gesicht war ganz rot von Anstrengung; es zog sich nach der Mitte zu zusammen und manchmal hob sich zuckend das eine Augenlid. Aber das Auge darunter schien leer zu sein.

»Das nützt nichts«, sagte das junge Mädchen mit ihrer durchsichtigen, von aufgelöstem Lachen glänzenden Stimme, »man kann nicht aufwachen, wenn die Augen noch nicht zurück sind.«

Ich wollte fragen; wie meinte sie das? Aber auf einmal verstand ich. Natürlich. Ich erinnerte mich eines jungen russischen Arbeiters vom Lande, der, als er nach Moskau kam, noch der Meinung war, die Sterne seien die Augen Gottes und die Augen der Engel. Man hat es ihm ausgeredet. Widerlegen konnte man ja eigentlich nichts, aber ausreden. Und mit Recht. Denn es sind die Augen der Menschen, die aus den geschlossenen Lidern aufsteigen und klar werden und sich erholen. Darum sind auch über dem Lande, wo alle schlafen, alle Sterne und über der Stadt nur wenige, weil da so viele Unruhige sind,

From the Dream-Book
The Seventh, Eleventh, and Twenty-Sixth Dreams

THE SEVENTH DREAM

I was looking for the young girl. I found her in a long narrow room where it was just morning. She was sitting on a chair and smiling almost imperceptibly. Next to her, no more than a step away, was a second chair with a young man stiffly sitting on it. The two of them seemed to have spent the night like that.

The young girl stirred and gave me her hand by reaching it up high towards me. This hand was warm and felt somehow hardened. It was like holding a small animal which lives in the wild and has to take care of itself.

And now the young man stirred too. He was visibly trying to wake up; his face was contorted in an unpleasant and impatient way. The young girl turned a little to the side and was looking at him. His face was all red from the effort; it puckered up toward the middle and sometimes he raised a fluttering eyelid. But the eye socket underneath seemed empty.

"It's no use," the young girl said in her transparent voice, sparkling with intense laughter. "You can't wake up if your eyes aren't back yet."

I wanted to ask what she meant by that, but suddenly I understood. Of course. I remembered a young Russian laborer from the country, who, when he came to Moscow, still thought that stars were the eyes of God and the eyes of the angels. People talked him out of it. They couldn't actually disprove it, but they could talk him out of it. And they were right. Because stars are the eyes of human beings, eyes that rise up out of closed lids and convalesce and become clear. That's also why in the country, where everyone sleeps, it's all stars, and above the city there are only a few, because there are so many sleepless people there, people crying and people reading, people laughing and awake, who keep them.

Weinende und Lesende, Lachende und Wache, die sie behalten.

Dieses junge Mädchen hätte es dem Russen sagen müssen. Aber sie dachte längst an andere Dinge. Sie erzählte von jemandem, von einem Mädchen, begriff ich, die jetzt in Meran verheiratet war. Sie heiß jetzt........, und belustigt nannte sie einen Namen. Ich nickte, nickte vielleicht zu sehr. »Nun weißt du natürlich etwas«, sagte sie spöttisch. »Daß ihr immer nach den Namen fragt und euch um Namen kümmert und tut, als wäre das was.« »Liebe«, sagte ich ernsthaft, »das hat auch Sinn bei den Menschen. Die Rosen heißen *Marie Baumann* oder *Madame Testout* oder *Gräfin von Camondo* oder *Emotion*, aber das ist beinahe überflüssig. Sie wissen ihre Namen nicht. Man hängt ihnen ein kleines Holztäfelchen an und sie nehmen es nicht ab. Das ist alles. Die Menschen aber wissen ihre Namen; sie interessieren sich dafür, wie sie heißen, sie lernen sie sorgfältig auswendig und sagen sie jedem, der danach fragt. Sie ernähren sie sozusagen ihr ganzes Leben und werden ihnen am Ende sehr ähnlich, zum Verwechseln, bis auf eine Kleinigkeit –«

Aber ich redete umsonst. Das junge Mädchen hörte nicht zu. Sie war aufgestanden, stand am Fenster, wo es schon Tag war, lächelte und rief jemanden. Einen Vogel, glaube ich.

DER ELFTE TRAUM

Dann war es eine Straße. Wir gingen zusammen hinab, in gleichem Schritt, nahe aneinander. Ihr Arm lag um meine Schultern.

Die Straße war breit, morgendlich leer, ein Boulevard, der ein wenig abfiel, sich neigte, gerade soviel als nottut, um dem Schritt eines Kindes sein bißchen Schwere zu nehmen. Sie ging als ob kleine Flügel an ihren Füßen wären.

Ich erinnerte mich –

»Woran erinnertest du dich –?« fragte sie nach einer Weile.

»Ich erinnerte mich –« sagte ich langsam, ohne das junge Mädchen anzusehen, »ich erinnerte mich einer Straße fern in einer östlichen Stadt, die ebenso breit war, ebenso leer, ebenso hell, nur viel, viel steiler war sie. Ich saß in einem kleinen Wagen.

This young girl must have been the one who told the Russian. But she's been thinking about other things for a long time now. She told the story of someone – a girl, I understood – who just got married in Merano. Now her name is . . . ., and she said, amused, a name. I nodded, nodded too much perhaps. "Now of course you know something," she said, making fun of me. "You all ask about names all the time, and worry about names, and act like they matter." "Love," I said seriously, "they do mean something with human beings. Roses are called Marie Baumann or Madame Testout or Countess de Camondo or Emotion, but it's practically superfluous. The roses don't know their names. We hang a little wooden nameplate around them and they don't take it off. That's it. But people, they know their names; they care what their names are; they carefully learn their names by heart and tell them to anyone who asks. They nourish their names, so to speak, for their whole lives and in the end they become just like their names, interchangeable except for some small detail – "

But I was talking for no reason. The young girl wasn't listening. She had stood up, she stood by the window, where it was already day, she smiled and called someone. A bird, I think.

The Eleventh Dream

Then there was a street. We walked down the street together, in step, next to each other. Her arm was around my shoulder. The street was wide, empty in the early morning, a boulevard that sloped down a little, just enough of an incline to take the little bit of weight off a child's footsteps. She walked as though there were tiny wings on her feet.

I remembered –

"What did you remember – ?" she asked after a while.

"I remembered – " I said slowly, without looking at the young girl, "I remembered a street, far away in an eastern city, which was just as wide as this one, just as empty, just as bright, only it was much, much steeper. I was sitting in a small carriage.

Das Pferd davor hatte eben alles auf sich genommen. Ich zweifelte nicht mehr: es fing an, durchzugehen. Der Kutscher gebärdete sich dementsprechend. Er nahm sich von hinten aus, als hätte er keinen Kopf mehr, und an seinem riesigen Rücken wurde gerissen wie an einem Knoten, den ein Zorniger auflösen will und der immer dichter sich zusammenzieht.

Der kleine Wagen raste, als risse er den Weg mit und die Häuser und alles, und als bliebe nichts hinter ihm stehen. Und unten, am Ende der Straße, war der Fluß, ein prächtiger selbstbewußter berühmter Fluß und glänzte. Ich sah, wie hell er war. Dann sah ich den Himmel voll von Morgen und hohen lebhaften Winden. Dann sah ich wieder den Kutscherrumpf, der alles verdeckte. Ich bildete mir ein, daß er schrie, aber über dem Lärm des Wagens war das nicht zu entscheiden. Wieder sah ich den Himmel, der einen wirklich schönen Tag versprach; und plötzlich erblickte ich für einen Augenblick das Pferd, ein gespenstisches Tier, viel zu groß für uns, und ich gewann fast die Überzeugung, daß es gar nicht zu uns gehörte. Ich sah, als ob ich Zeit hätte, ein Kind in einer Türe, still spielend. Ich sah eine Kneipe an einer Straßenecke; neben der Tür, auf einem Blechschild, war eine Flasche gemalt, eine kleine, krumme, dicke, sonderbare Flasche; es war höchst zweifelhaft, ob es überhaupt so eine Flasche gab. Ein Fenster blendete mich, das irgendwo aufgegangen war; dann sah ich den Bruchteil einer Sekunde lang ein entsetztes Gesicht und dann . . . .

Aber nur so weit erinnerte ich mich.«

»Ich weiß, warum du dich erinnertest–« sagte das junge Mädchen.

»Ja, weil wir gehen. Und weil mir damals in jenen seltsam ausführlichen Augenblicken, in denen ich eine Menge sah, sehr ähnlich zu Mute war. Als ob es im Grunde dasselbe wäre; dasselbe Gefühl, dieselbe Welle von Gefühlen, Dingen, Gedanken, Glanz und Bewegung, die alles mitreißt . . .«

»Merkwürdig seid ihr«, sagte das junge Mädchen, während wir immer so weitergingen die breite helle Straße hinab. »Ihr denkt, ihr tut fast nichts anderes, und doch entgeht euch alles. Hast du noch gar nicht gewußt, daß die Freude ein Schrecken

The horse pulling the carriage was getting all worked up. And then I was sure of it: and the horse bolted. The coachman conducted himself accordingly. From behind, it looked like he had no head, and his giant back was being yanked like a knot that you angrily want to untie and that only pulls itself tighter and tighter.

"The little carriage raced ahead like a hurricane sweeping away the road and the houses and everything else, as though nothing would be left standing behind it. Down below, at the end of the street, was the river, a magnificent, confident, famous river, and it sparkled. I looked at how bright it was. Then I looked at the sky, full of morning and lively high winds. Then I looked at the coachman's body again, which blocked everything. I imagined he was yelling but there was no way to tell over the noise of the carriage. Again I looked at the sky, which promised a truly beautiful day; and suddenly I caught a glimpse of the horse for a second, a spooky animal like some kind of spirit, much too big for us, and I almost believed that it didn't belong to us at all. I looked – as though I had time to look – at a child in a doorway, playing quietly. I looked at a bar on a streetcorner; there was a bottle painted on a tin sign near the door, a small, crooked, thick, bizarre bottle; it was highly unlikely that there had ever been or ever would be a bottle like that. A window blinded me, being swung open somewhere; then I saw for a split second a horrified face and then. . . .

"But that's all I remember."

"I know why you remembered that – " the young girl said.

"Yes, because we're walking. And because I felt very similar then, in those strangely detailed moments when I saw so much. As though it were, in essence, the same: the same feeling, the same waves of feelings, things, thoughts, sparkle and motion sweeping everything away. . ."

"You are all so strange," the young girl said, as we kept walking down the wide, bright street. "You think, you do almost nothing but think, but none of you get anything. Didn't you have any idea that joy is a terrible fright that we're not afraid of? We go through a terrible fright, right through to the end, and

ist, vor dem man keine Furcht hat? Man geht durch einen Schrecken durch bis ans Ende: und das ist eben die Freude. Ein Schrecken, von dem man nicht nur den Anfangsbuchstaben kennt. Ein Schrecken, zu dem man Vertrauen hat. – Oder hattest du Angst?«

»Ich weiß es nicht«, sagte ich verwirrt. »Ich kann dir nicht antworten.«

Der sechsundzwanzigste Traum

»– Hier fortgenommen und unter einen Glassturz gestellt –« sagte das junge Mädchen, in das Nebenzimmer zurückgewendet. Dann kam sie ganz herein und schloß die Türe, indem sie sie leise an sich zog.

»Claire –« sagte ich unter dem Zwange des Gefühls, daß alles schon einmal genau so gewesen war; damals mußte man Claire sagen an der Stelle. Aber diesmal zweigte es ab, und zwar so sehr, daß alles zu sagen erlaubt gewesen wäre: Kobalt oder Atemlosigkeit oder Karausche, nur nicht das, nur nicht: Claire. Es war falsch, es war verletzend, es war geradezu unmöglich, in diesem Augenblicke Claire zu sagen.

Ich begriff das sofort und verstand es so völlig, daß die Verachtung, mit der das junge Mädchen sich von mir abkehrte, nichts Überraschendes für mich hatte. Ich hörte sie irgendwo eine Lade aufziehen, und etwas später stand sie mit einem Stück Hand-Arbeit am Fenster, hielt es ins Licht, spannte es und sah es mit etwas schief geneigtem Kopfe an. Und so, in dieser Stellung, sagte sie geringschätzend: »Es ist unbegreiflich, daß Sie sie nicht küssen wollten.«

Das war nun eine ganz haltlose Stichelei, und ich begnügte mich mit einer kleinen ironischen Gebärde. Das junge Mädchen setzte sich auf das breite Fensterbrett, legte das Stück Hand-Arbeit über das eine Knie und strich es langsam, nach rechts und nach links, mit beiden Händen glatt. Und unter dem Einfluß dieses Streichens oder wie ich so das blonde gesenkte Haar des jungen Mädchens betrachte oder weiß Gott bei

then it's just joy. A terror we don't even know the first letter of. A terror we know deeply, and trust. – Or were you scared?"

"I don't know," I said, confused. "I can't answer you."

The Twenty-Sixth Dream

"– Taken away from here and put under a glass cover – " the young girl said, turning around to the other room. Then she came in entirely and shut the door by softly pulling it toward her.

"Claire – " I said, under the compulsion of feeling that everything was exactly like it had been once before. Back then, one had to say *Claire*. But this time it branched off, so strongly that I could have said anything here – *cobalt* or *breathlessness* or *koi* – just not that, not: *Claire*. It was wrong, it was painful, it was absolutely impossible to say *Claire* at this moment.

I understood immediately, and so completely that the contempt with which the young girl turned away from me didn't surprise me in the least. I heard her pull open a drawer somewhere and a bit later she was standing at the window with a piece of needlework in her hands, holding it up to the light, spreading it out and looking at it with her head slightly tilted. And then, in that position, she said, as though it meant nothing to her: "It makes no sense that you didn't want to kiss her."

Now that attack came out of nowhere, and I made do with a small ironic gesture. The young girl sat down on the broad windowsill, lay the piece of needlework over her knee, and slowly stroked it, to the right, to the left, smoothed it out with both hands. And under the influence of this stroking, or of how I was observing the blond lowered hair of the young girl, or God knows why, I realize that it truly does make no sense. A gigantic incomprehensibility comes out at me from a small

welchem Anlaß, merke ich wirklich, daß es unbegreiflich ist. Eine riesige Unbegreiflichkeit kommt auf mich zu aus einer kleinen Erinnerung. Ich sehe Augen, die vergrößerten Augen einer Schwindsüchtigen, und diese Augen baten. Lieber Gott, was baten diese Augen.

»Nun wird nicht viel mehr da sein von ihr«, sagte das junge Mädchen. Ihre beiden Hände lagen nebeneinander über der Arbeit auf dem Knie, und es war, als entfernte sie sich so weit als möglich von ihnen, wie sie sich nun zurückneigte und mich ansah. Sie sah mich an, aber sie machte ihren Blick so weit, daß ich darin gleichsam alle Konturen verlor.

»Sie war ein Dienstmädchen«, sagte ich hastig, wie auf eine Frage, und als wäre das der letzte Moment für eine solche Aussprache. Und ich wußte gar nicht, daß ich von da ab erzählte:

»Sie war (muß ich erzählt haben) in dem großen Hôtel, wo meistens Kranke wohnten. Ich blieb übrigens kaum acht Tage da. Sie bediente mich. Es fiel mir auf, daß sie mich gut bediente; sie wußte am dritten Tage alles, kannte meine kleinen Gewohnheiten, verwöhnte sie. Aber sie hustete. Sie hatte sich angesteckt. ›Sie husten‹, sagte ich einmal am Morgen. Sie lächelte nur. Gleich darauf, draußen, packte es sie von neuem.

Dann reiste ich. In Florenz, als ich meinen Koffer öffnete, war das eine Fach ganz mit Veilchen bedeckt. Und am Abend flatterte ein kleiner Zettel aus meinem Nachtzeug. Lebe wohl, stand darauf. Wie in der Schule nach Diktat geschrieben.

Natürlich dachte ich nicht wieder an sie. Doch; als ich zwei Monate später wieder in das große Hôtel kam, wo meistens Kranke wohnten, und sie war nicht da, fragte ich sogar nach ihr. ›Die Marie ist krank‹, sagte das fremde Stubenmädchen gleichsam beleidigt. Aber am Abend war sie da. Es war April, und das Klima des Ortes war berühmt. An diesem Abend aber war es merkwürdig kalt. Sie kniete an meinem Ofen, und als ihr Gesicht sich mir zuwandte, kam es aus dem Feuerschein. Ihre Augen glänzten vom Feuer. Sie stand nicht gleich auf, und ich bemerkte, daß es ihr schwer wurde aufzustehen. Ich half ihr ein wenig. Ich fühlte, wie leicht sie war. ›Geht es gut, ja?‹ sagte ich nachlässig und wie mit einem Wunsch nach Lustigkeit. Sie gab

memory. I see eyes, the wide eyes of a consumptive, and they plead. Dear God, what these eyes plead.

"Well there won't be much left of her now," the young girl said. Her hands lay next to each other on top of the handiwork on her knee, and when she straightened back up and looked at me it was as if she was distancing herself from these hands as far as possible. She looked at me but she made her gaze so wide that it was as if I lost all outlines in it.

"She was a maid," I said in a hurry, as though answering a question, and as if this were the last possible moment to say such a thing. And without realizing it I started the story from there:

"She was," I must have said, "in the grand hôtel that's mostly for sick people. I was there barely a week, by the way. She was my maid. I noticed that she served me well; by the third day she knew everything, all my little habits, and indulged them. But she had a cough. She had caught something. 'You have a cough,' I said one morning. She only smiled. Right after that, outside the room, it took hold of her again.

"Then I left on a trip. In Florence, when I opened my suitcase, one compartment was entirely covered in violets. And that evening a little slip of paper fluttered out of my overnight bag. *Farewell*, it said. Like something written down from dictation in school.

"Naturally I didn't think about her again. But still – when I came back, two months later, to the grand hôtel that's mostly for sick people, and she wasn't there, I did in fact ask after her. 'Marie, she's sick,' said the new chambermaid, as though insulted. But in the evening she was there. It was April, and the climate of the place was famous. But on this evening it was unusually cold. She knelt down in front of my heater and as her face turned toward me it emerged from the glow of the fire. Her eyes sparkled from the fire. She didn't stand up right away and I noticed that it had become hard for her to stand up. I helped her a little. I felt how light she was. 'Everything's all right, yes?' I said carelessly, as though I was trying to be cheerful. She didn't answer, I remember; she just looked at me, looked at me,

keine Antwort, erinnere ich mich; sie sah mich nur an, sah mich an, sah mich an. Nicht von ganz nahe mehr; sie war bis an den Schrank zurückgetreten. Ich glaube es war ihr schwer, zu stehen. Die Dämmerung im Zimmer nahm keine Rücksicht auf uns. Es dunkelte. Es war nichts da, was die Sache erleichtern mochte. Und sie hatte es ganz allein, das Schwere. Denn ich war damals nur verlegen und beunruhigt, ja und ungeduldig. Schließlich aber hatte sie überwunden, kam (sie hatte noch Kraft, immer wieder noch Kraft), kam und sah mich nochmals von ganz nahe an. Wie dunkel es war. Es schien mir, als wäre ihr Haar weicher geworden, durch die Krankheit vielleicht oder weil sie nicht mehr gedient hatte in der letzten Zeit. Sie hob ein bißchen die Arme (das hätte ich beinahe vergessen) und legte mir beide Hände flach auf die Brust. Das war das Letzte ehe sie ging –«

Hier erschrak ich. »Habe ich jetzt immerzu gesprochen?« fragte ich beunruhigt nach dem jungen Mädchen hinüber. Ich sah sie erst gar nicht; sie saß in einem großen grün bezogenen Lehnstuhl, der früher noch nicht neben dem Fenster gestanden hatte. Sie saß über ihre Arbeit gebeugt, ein klein wenig mehr möglicherweise als nötig war.

»Und du?« sagte sie plötzlich. Sie sah nicht einmal auf.

»Ich, ja, – ich ließ sie gehen. Ich tat nichts. Ich sagte auch nichts. Ich suchte nach etwas Unverfänglichem, Belanglosem –«

Das junge Mädchen blickte auf, prüfend, mit jener verwirrenden Dunkelheit im Schauen, die sich in manchen blauen Augen bildet, wenn sie eine Zeit lang gesenkt bleiben.

»Und dann?« fragte sie.

»Dann machte ich Licht.«

Sie war schon wieder beschäftigt. Sie wendete ihre Arbeit nach rechts und nach links, hielt sie dann von sich ab und betrachtete sie, den Kopf zurückgebogen, aus möglichst großer Entfernung mit halbgeschlossenen Augen.

»Ich ging wohl bald zu Ruh«, fiel mir ein, »ich war müde. Oder nein, ich las noch; richtig, ich las –«

Und ich hoffte im Stillen mich zu besinnen, was ich damals wohl noch gelesen haben könnte.

Sie aber legte mit kurzem Entschluß und ohne viel

looked at me. Not from right up close any more; she had retreated back to the armoire. I think it was hard for her to stand. The twilight in the room took no account of us. It got dark. There was nothing there to make things easier. She had it, the difficult burden, all alone – I was only embarrassed and worried, impatient too. But at last she prevailed, came closer (she still had some strength left, even then), came closer and looked at me again from close up. How dark it was. It seemed to me that her hair had gotten softer, maybe because of her illness or because she hadn't been working recently. She lifted her arms a little (I had almost forgotten that) and placed her hands flat on my chest. That was the last thing before she left – "

Here I started with fright. "Have I been talking this whole time?" I worriedly asked the young girl across from me. I didn't even see her at first; she was sitting in a large green covered armchair, which wasn't there by the window before, bent over her needlework possibly a slight bit more than was necessary.

"And you?" she said suddenly. She didn't look up once.

"Me, yes, well – I let her go. I didn't do anything. I didn't say anything either. I was looking for something harmless, something trivial, no strings attached – "

The young girl glanced up, questioning, with that bewildering darkness in her look which appears in certain blue eyes when they've been lowered for a while.

"And then?" she asked.

"Then I turned on the light."

She was already busy with her needlework again. She turned it to the right, to the left, then held it down in front of her and examined it with half-closed eyes, with her head bent back, from the greatest possible distance.

"I must have gone to bed right away," it occured to me, "I was tired. Or no, I was still reading; that's right, I was reading – "

I hoped I would be able to consider the matter in private and remember what I might have been reading.

But she, with quick decisiveness and without being very careful, it seemed to me, put her needlework down on the window -

Sorgfalt, kam mir vor, die Arbeit auf das Fensterbrett und suchte einige bunte Fäden zusammen, die in ihrem Schooße geblieben waren. »Lasest«, sagte sie auf einmal höhnisch und sah rasch auf mit ganz kalten undurchsichtigen Augen. »Lasest –« wiederholte sie mit unbeschreiblicher Härte.

Das Wort, wie sie es sagte, verlor seinen Sinn. Mir war, als hätte sie den Namen einer Krankheit genannt, die gerade herrscht, einer ansteckenden Krankheit, an der viele sterben. Mich durchschauerte es, als ob sie mich eben ergriffen hätte.

Das junge Mädchen hatte jetzt die Hände um das eine hochgezogene Knie gefaltet; ihr Gesicht war weggewendet, dem Fenster zu, und dort irgendwo hinaus sagte sie: »Lieber Gott –« mit dem Ton auf der ersten langen Silbe.

Schließlich ertrug ich es nicht mehr. Ich tat ein paar Schritte auf das Fenster zu. Ich fühlte, wie in mir Worte entstanden, die ich nur sagen mußte, um –

Da erhoben sich Stimmen im Nebenzimmer. Es war, als würde ein ganzes Bündel durcheinandergeratener Stimmen gegen die Tür geworfen, und noch ein Mal, – und wir standen beide da, wie mir schien, in der gleichen Angst.

sill and collected up a few bright threads that had been left behind on her lap. "Reading," she said, suddenly scornful, and she looked up quickly with utterly cold, opaque eyes. "Reading – " she repeated in an indescribably hard voice.

The word lost its meaning the way she said it. It felt like she was saying the name of a disease, an epidemic in fact, an infectious disease lots of people were dying of. A shudder ran through me, as though the disease had overcome me too. Then the young girl had folded her hands on a raised knee; her face was turned away, to the window, and she said to someone or something outside the window there "Dear God – " emphasizing the long first syllable.

At last I couldn't stand it any more. I took a few steps toward the window. I felt words rise up within me, words I had only to say in order to –

Then voices were raised in the other room. It was as though a whole cluster of voices all mixed together had been thrown against the door, then thrown again – and we stood there, gripped, it seemed to me, by the same fear.

[Eine Morgenandacht]

Steh froh auf zu deinem Werktage, wenn du es kannst. Und kannst du es nicht, was hindert dich daran? Ist da etwas Schweres im Wege? Was hast du gegen das Schwere? Daß es dich töten kann. Es ist also mächtig und stark. Das weißt du von ihm. Und was weißt du vom Leichten? Nichts. An das Leichte haben wir gar keine Erinnerung. Selbst wenn du also wählen dürftest, müßtest du nicht eigentlich das Schwere wählen? Fühlst du nicht, wie verwandt es mit dir ist? Ist es nicht durch alle deine Lieben mit dir verwandt? Ist es nicht das eigentlich Heimatliche?

Und bist du nicht im Einklang mit der Natur, wenn du es wählst? Meinst du, dem Keim wäre es nicht leichter in der Erde zu bleiben? Oder haben es die Zugvögel nicht schwer, und die wilden Tiere, die für sich sorgen müssen?

Sieh: es giebt gar nicht ein Leichtes und ein Schweres. Das Leben selbst ist das Schwere. Und leben willst du doch? Du irrst also, wenn du das Pflicht nennst, daß du das Schwere auf dich nimmst. Es ist Selbsterhaltungstrieb, was dich dazu drängt. Was aber ist denn Pflicht? Pflicht ist das Schwere zu lieben. Daß du es trägst will wenig sagen, du mußt es wiegen und einsingen und du mußt da sein, wenn es dich braucht. Und es kann dich jeden Augenblick brauchen.

So groß muß deine Hilfsbereitschaft und deine Güte sein, daß du es verwöhnst, dein Schweres, daß es nicht sein kann ohne dich, daß es von dir abhängig wird wie ein Kind.

Hast du es erst so weit gebracht, so wirst du nicht wollen, daß jemand komme und es dir abnähme.

Und du bringst es so weit durch die Liebe. Lieben ist schwer. Und wenn einer dich lieben heißt, so giebt er dir eine große Aufgabe; aber keine unmögliche. Denn er heißt dich nicht einen Menschen lieben, was nichts für Anfänger ist, und er verlangt nicht von dir, daß du Gott lieben sollst, was nur die Reifsten können. Er weist dich nur auf dein Schweres hin, welches dein Dürftigstes ist und dein Fruchtbarstes zugleich. Das Leichte, siehst du, will nichts von dir; aber das Schwere wartet auf dich,

Morning Prayer

On work days arise to your labors happily, if you can. And if you can't, what's stopping you? Is there something heavy, something difficult in your way? What do you have against what's heavy and difficult? –That it can kill you. –Alright, so it's strong and powerful, you know that much about it. And what do you know about what's easy? Nothing. We have no memory at all of what's easy. So even if you were permitted to choose, wouldn't you actually have to choose what's hard? Don't you feel how kindred it is to you, related to you through all your loves? Is it not your true home?

And aren't you in harmony with nature when you choose it? Don't you think the seed would find it easier to stay in the earth? Don't the migrating birds have it hard, and the wild animals who have to fend for themselves?

Look: easy things and hard things simply do not exist. Life itself is what's hard. And you want to live, don't you? So you're wrong to call it your duty to take on what's hard. The survival instinct pushes you to do that. So what is your duty? Your duty is to love what's hard. That you carry the weight doesn't say much, you have to rock it in its cradle and sing it to sleep and be there when it needs you, and it can need you at any moment.

You have to be so ready to help, so gentle and kind, that you spoil it, spoil your difficult thing like a child, so that it can no longer exist without you, so that it depends on you.

After you've brought it to such a state you will no longer want anyone to come take it off your hands.

And you get that far through love. To love is hard. When someone bids you to love, they are laying a great task upon you, but not an impossible one. For they are not calling you to love another person, which is not for beginners; they are not demanding from you that you love God, which only the most mature people can do. They are only calling your attention to what's hard for you, what is neediest in you and at the same time most fruitful. You see, what's easy wants nothing from you, but what's

und du hast keine Kraft, die da nicht nötig wäre, und, auch wenn dein Leben sehr lang ist, bleibt dir kein Tag für das Leichte übrig, das deiner spottet.

Geh hinein in dich und baue an deinem Schweren. Dein Schweres soll sein wie ein Haus in dir, wenn du selbst wie ein Land bist, das sich mit den Gezeiten verändert. Gedenke, daß du kein Stern bist: du hast keine Bahn.

Du mußt für dich selbst eine Welt sein und dein Schweres muß in deiner Mitte sein und dich anziehen. Und eines Tages wird es wirken über dich hinaus mit seiner Schwerkraft auf ein Schicksal, auf einen Menschen, auf Gott. Dann kommt Gott in dein Schweres wenn es fertig ist. Und welche Stelle wüßtest du sonst, um mit ihm zusammenzukommen?

hard waits for you, and there is no strength in you that won't be needed there, and even if your life is very long not a single day will be left over for what's easy, what scoffs at your strength.

Go deep inside yourself and build what's hard. It should be like a house within you, if you yourself are like a land that changes with the tides. Remember, you are not a star, you have no course to follow.

You must be a world unto yourself and with your difficult thing in your center, drawing you to it. And one day, with its weight, its gravity, it will have its effects beyond you, on a destiny, on a person, on God. Then, when it's ready, God will enter into your difficult thing. And do you know anywhere else where you and He can meet?

Durch den sich Vögel werfen, ist nicht der
vertraute Raum, der die Gestalt dir steigert.
(Im Freien, dorten, bist du dir verweigert
und schwindest weiter ohne Wiederkehr.)

Raum greift aus uns und übersetzt die Dinge:
daß dir das Dasein eines Baums gelinge,
wirf Innenraum um ihn, aus jenem Raum,
der in dir west. Umgieb ihn mit Verhaltung.
Er grenzt sich nicht. Erst in der Eingestaltung
in dein Verzichten wird er wirklich Baum.

What birds hurtle through is not the familiar sky
that raises form and shape within you.
(Out in the open, out there, you are denied
to yourself and fade, fade farther, forever.)

Sky grabs out from us and translates things:
that you might reach a tree in all its being
fling inner sky around it, from that sky
that abides in you. Ring it with measure.
It will not edge itself. Only the pressure
in your renouncing makes it truly tree.

1875   René Karl Wilhelm Johann Josef Maria Rilke is born on December 4, in Prague, to unhappily married parents. He is an only child, though a year before a girl had been born and died after only a few weeks; this lost sister shapes his childhood, as his mother dresses him in girls' clothes for much longer than was usual at the time and encourages him to play the role of a daughter in games with her.

Parents separate (1884). Military school, which Rilke hates (1886–91, leaves due to illness). Publishes first two books of poetry (1894, 1895). University in Prague (1895) and Munich (1896).

1897   Meets and becomes the lover of Lou Andreas-Salomé – fifteen years older than Rilke, already the author of two novels and studies of Ibsen and Nietzsche, a former lover of Nietzsche's, future disciple of Freud's, and the person who more than anyone else would shape Rilke's identity as an artist. She convinces him to change his name to the more masculine "Rainer" and to travel to Italy, teaches him Russian and brings him to Russia for two influential trips (1899, 1900), introduces him to Tolstoy, and even after they stop being lovers in 1900 is a crucial correspondent and mentor for the rest of his life.

1899   Writes in a single autumn night the draft of what would later be published as *The Lay of the Love and Death of Cornet Christoph Rilke*, about an ancestor who died in the Austro-Turkish War of 1660. Published in 1906, republished in 1912, it is by far Rilke's most popular work during his life, especially during World War I – 200,000 copies were sold by 1920 and over a million by 1960, astronomical figures for the time.

1900   Second trip to Russia with Salomé ends with the collapse of their relationship in August. Travels to the artist colony of Worpswede, in northwest Germany, where he meets and

becomes close with both Clara Westhoff, a sculptor, and Paula Becker, a painter. Leaves unexpectedly one night, barely a month later, possibly after he finds out that Paula is engaged to the painter Otto Modersohn.

1901   Is Clara's lover by February; they marry on April 28; their only child Ruth is born on December 12.

1902   Moves to Paris in August to become Auguste Rodin's secretary in his country home in Meudon. Having used Clara to approach Rodin, he uses Rodin and his slogan "Work, always work," to convince Clara that they must live apart, leave Ruth with relatives in Germany, that in general he must always follow what he describes as the dictates of his art. They are poor; Rilke supports Clara and Ruth when he can, and occasionally lives with them during the next few years, but never fully accepts the duties of being a husband and father.

At the end of his life, for example, he writes to the poet Marina Tsvetaeva: "almost the only time I really was with [my daughter] was before any verbalness at all, from her birth to sometime after her first birthday: for as early as that, what had arisen, a little against my will, in terms of house, family, and settling down, was dissolving; the marriage, too, although never terminated legally, returned me to my natural singleness (after barely two years) and Paris began: this was 1902."

1903   Publishes the study *Auguste Rodin*; writes letters that would later be published as *Letters to a Young Poet*; stays with a succession of patrons and patronnesses, including Rodin, a pattern which he would continue for the rest of his life.

1906   Is fired by Rodin; publishes the second, expanded *Book of Pictures* (or *Book of Images*); writes the poems of his great book *New Poems*; continues work on his novel of Paris, *The Notebooks of Malte Laurids Brigge*. Spends an intense month with Paula Modersohn-Becker, possibly as lovers, and sits for a portrait while she is in Paris, separated from her husband.

1907   Writes *Letters on Cézanne* to Clara but in a way intended primarily for Paula; *New Poems* is published; Paula Modersohn-Becker dies shortly after giving birth.

1908   A second part of *New Poems* is published; Rilke writes his great poem "Requiem" for Paula Modersohn-Becker, finishing it on All Souls' Day (November 2), always a meaningful day of remembrance for him.

  Notebooks of Malte Laurids Brigge is published (1910). Stays at Duino Castle (Oct. 1911–May 1912), where he writes half of the *Duino Elegies* after hearing the first line come to him in a voice from the air as he walked along a sea cliff – "Who, if I cried out, would hear me among the hierarchies of the angels?" Rilke's inability to finish this major work is the creative crisis of the next decade of his life.

1914   Is surprised in Germany when World War I is declared, and is unable to return to Paris; stuck, mostly in Munich, for the duration of the war, he is anxious and severely depressed, serving briefly in the military (not in combat) in 1916. Eventually leaves for Switzerland (1919), and stays for long periods at houses and castles put at his disposal by the patrons he cultivated.

1921   Finds permanent residence in the solitary small château at Muzot, in Switzerland, where he would live rent-free, often in ill health, for the rest of his life, except for stays at Val-Mont sanatorium (1924, 1925, 1926) and travels to Paris (Jan.–Aug. 1925) and elsewhere.

1922   In three weeks (February 2–23), writes the rest of the *Duino Elegies* and the entire *Sonnets to Orpheus* sequence of fifty-five poems. Feels that his life's work is complete, and the last years of his life are noticeably happier and more content. Continues to write and translate, including a large body of poetry in French.

1926   Dies December 29, of leukemia.

Because the poems, notes, and dreams in this volume are not in chronological order, it may be useful to list them here, to give an overview of their development and the periods in Rilke's life from which certain clusters arose.

1898
Interiors and *Notes on the Melody of Things*

1899–1900
Spring Songs (II), *Vitali Awoke*, *Night Songs* (II), and *When Death Came with the Morning*

1903
On Completing the Circle (I)

1905
Marriage and *Morning Prayer*

1906
The Lady and the Unicorn and *"There is total silence. . ."*

1907 (Jan.–Feb.)
From the Notebooks (*Naples* and *Capri*), *From the Dream-Book*, and *Dream* (*Fragment*)

1907 (Autumn)
From the Notebooks (*Paris*) and *Young Girl*

1908–1911
The Origin of the Chimera, *Pregnant Woman*, and *Night Songs* (I)

1913–1916
In His Thirty-Eighth Year, *"Looking up from the book, from the near and countable lines,"* *Note on Birds*, and *"It's not that now that we're (suddenly) grown up"*

1919–1921
Introduction to a Poetry Reading, Haiku (I), and *Testament*

1922 (Jan. 31)
"As long as you catch what you've thrown yourself"

1923–early 1924
On the Poet's Material, On Completing the Circle (II), *On Shawls and Lemons* (I–III), and *Spring Songs* (I)

1924 (June–July)
"What birds hurtle through is not the familiar sky," On Shawls and Lemons (IV), and *Poems from the Graveyard*

1926
Dedication, Haiku (II), and *"Come then, come, you last thing I have learned"*

Notes

All texts in this book and many of the notes below are taken from the six-volume *Sämtliche Werke* [Complete Works] of Rainer Maria Rilke (Insel, 1965); *Die Briefe an Gräfin Sizzo: 1921–1926* [Letters to Countess Sizzo] (Insel, 1950); or *Das Testament* [Testament] (Insel, 1975).

"As long as you can catch what you've thrown yourself"
Muzot, January 31, 1922.

Two days later – February 2 – began the incomparable burst of creativity, or receptivity, which produced twenty-five Sonnets to Orpheus in three days and the entire *Sonnets to Orpheus* (fifty-five poems) and half of *The Duino Elegies* by February 23. See the Translator's Afterword for more on this poem.

Pregnant Woman
Paris, summer of 1909. One of three unfinished drafts.

Interiors
Probably fall of 1898; unpublished in Rilke's lifetime. In 1898, Rilke was twenty-two years old.

Young Girl
Paris, fall 1907.

The Lady and the Unicorn
Paris, June 9, 1906.

Rilke describes the Lady and the Unicorn tapestries at greater length in his novel *The Notebooks of Malte Laurids Brigge*, at the end of Part One and the start of Part Two. Abelone is Malte's mother's youngest sister, whom he loves one summer under a goldenrain tree:

There are tapestries here, Abelone, tapestries on the wall.
I imagine you here, there are six tapestries, come, let us walk

slowly past them. But first step back and look at them all at once. How calm, how quiet they are, don't you think? There is not much variation in them. It is always the same blue oval island floating on a muted red background that is flowery and inhabited by small animals busy amongst themselves. Only there, in the last tapestry, does the island rise a little higher, as though grown lighter. It always bears a figure, a woman, in a different costume each time but always the same woman. A smaller figure is next to her at times, a servant, and the animals bearing the coat of arms are always there, large, with her on the island, in the action. On the left, a lion; on the right, bright white, the unicorn; they hold the same pennants, high above them, that show: three silver moons, rising, in a blue band on a red ground. – Are you done looking? Shall we begin with the first?

She is feeding the falcon. How splendid her dress is. The bird is on her gloved hand and it moves. She looks at it while reaching into the dish that her servant has brought her for something to give it. To the right, down on her train, stands a small, silk-haired dog, looking up and hoping they'll remember something for him. And, did you notice, a low rose trellis runs along the back of the island. The animals rear up, heraldically proud. The coat of arms envelops each of them a second time, as a cape. A beautiful agraffe clasps it closed. The wind blows.

We move to the next tapestry in involuntary silence, do we not? as soon as we realize how absorbed she is: she is binding a wreath, a small circular crown of flowers. Sunk in thought, she chooses the color of the next carnation in the shallow basin that the serving girl is holding for her, while she puts the previous one in its proper place. Behind her, on a bench, is an unused basket full of roses that a monkey has uncovered. It's carnations this time. The lion no longer takes part; on the right, the unicorn understands.

Mustn't music now enter into this silence, wasn't it already there, muted, and waiting? Heavily, silently adorned, she has stepped (how slowly, no?) to the portable organ and

she plays, standing, cut off by the pipework from the serving girl working the bellows on the other side. She has never been so beautiful. Her hair has been wound into two wondrous braids and brought forward, reuniting on top of her headdress, so that the ends rise up out of the knot like a short plume on a helmet. The lion is out of tune with the moment, disgruntled, unhappily enduring the notes and stifling a howl. The unicorn, though, is beautiful, swaying as if on the waves.

The island grows wider. A tent has been pitched, of blue damask emblazoned with gold. The animals gather up the opening and she steps forth, in a lavish dress but simply, almost, because what are her pearls compared to her. The serving girl has opened a small chest and now she lifts a string of jewels out of it, a heavy, priceless treasure which has always been locked away. The little dog sits near her raised up, on a prepared place, and looks on. And have you discovered the words on the top edge of the tent? Written there is: "A mon seul désir."

What has happened, why is the little rabbit hopping down below, why do we see right away that it is hopping? Everything is so awkward. The lion has nothing to do. She holds the banner herself. Or is she holding on to it? She has grasped the unicorn's horn with her other hand. Is that mourning, can mourning stand so upright, can a mourning dress be as mute as this green-black velvet with its faded parts?

But there is still one more party. No one is invited to it, expectation plays no role. Everything is already there. Everything, for always. The lion looks around, almost threatening: no one may approach. We have never yet seen her tired – is she tired? or has she sat down only because she is bearing something heavy? A monstrance, one might think. But she bends her other arm toward the unicorn and the animal rears up, flattered, and climbs up and rests on her lap. It is a mirror she is holding. Look: she shows the unicorn its image –

Abelone, I imagine you here. Do you understand, Abelone? I think you must understand.

* * *

Now the Lady and the Unicorn tapestries, too, are no longer in the old Château de Boussac. The time has come when everything comes out of the houses, they cannot contain anything any longer. Danger has become safer than safety. No one from the race of the Delle Vistes accompanies one or has it in their blood. They are all long gone. No one speaks your name, Pierre d'Aubusson, the great grandmaster from the ancient house, at whose behest, perhaps, were woven these images that praise all and betray nothing. (Oh, why did poets ever write of women otherwise! They thought it was more literal. But surely we are not meant to know anything but this.) Now people come before them by chance, among others there by chance, and are almost terrified not to have been invited. But there are others there, walking past, if not many. The young people barely pause, unless their business somehow requires them to have seen these things once, to have noticed this or that particular characteristic.

Young girls, though, may be found standing before them from time to time. There are lots of young girls in the museums, who have come forth here and there from the houses that no longer contain anything. They find themselves in front of these tapestries and forget themselves a little. They have always felt that this existed, a quiet life like this, of slow, never quite explained gestures, and they darkly remember that they in fact thought, for a long while, that this would be their own lives. But then they quickly pull out a notebook and begin to sketch, it doesn't matter what, one of the flowers or a small, contented animal. It wouldn't make any difference whether or not someone had told them what exactly it is. And in truth it doesn't make any difference. The main thing is that a drawing be made, for that is why they came forth one day, with a certain violence.

ON COMPLETING THE CIRCLE (I): Works of Art
Paris, January 1903.

On Completing the Circle (II)

Muzot, from a letter to Countess Margot Sizzo (*née* Crouy-Chanel), January 6, 1923.

Rilke used his ancestral coat of arms, two greyhounds and a helmet, as the frontispiece for *The Lay of the Love and Death of Cornet Christoph Rilke*. It also makes an appearance in this early poem (from mid-October 1900), which I would like to preserve for English-speaking posterity as perhaps the single most pretentious poem Rilke ever wrote; jangly rhymes are in the original:

> I am an image.
> Don't ask me to speak.
> I am an image, too weak
> for any gesture.
> My life is the silence of the form.
> I am the birth and the death of the gesture.
> I am so old
> that I'll never grow older.
> Sometimes people stand near me at night
> and hold in front of my face a light
> and see just one thing: I am not it.
>
> My coat of arms rises high in the corner.
> The greyhound rears.
> And no one hears
> a sound from the heavy helmet's closed visor.

Rilke was correct that the painted arms did survive in the estate assembly hall in Klagenfurt, Austria, as indeed they still do, in a room painted with hundreds of coats of arms of the Austrian nobility. In fact, though, Rilke was not descended from the noble Rülke family, and the coat of arms is not his family's.

Dedication

Muzot, around June 26, 1926.

VITALI AWOKE
From Rilke's diary, Berlin–Schmargendorf, April 7, 1900.

NOTES ON THE MELODY OF THINGS
Probably fall of 1898, probably after "Interiors"; unpublished in
Rilke's lifetime.

In a reply to Rudolf Steiner's response to his essay "The
Value of the Monologue," from the same period, Rilke wrote:

> What I want on stage, in the space above and beside the
> words, are things in the broadest sense. To my mind, the
> stage does not have one wall (the fourth wall) too few to be
> "realistic," but rather three walls too many. I want space for
> everything that takes part in our days; everything that
> touches us, and determines us, from childhood on.
>
> These things are as much a part of us as words. As
> though the Dramatis Personæ were to include a cupboard,
> a glass, a sound, and the many finer, more delicate things
> too. In life they all have the same value: a thing is no worse
> than a word or a scent or a dream. On stage, too, this equal-
> ity will little by little become law, and justice will one day
> be done.
>
> It may well be that life flows along in words for a while
> like a river in its bed; but when it becomes free and pow-
> erful it broadens out and covers everything, and no one can
> see any longer where its banks lie.

HAIKU (I)
Geneva, early September 1920.

HAIKU (II)
Fall 1926.

POEMS FROM THE GRAVEYARD (I–V)
Ragaz, July 1–21, 1924.

These are poems I, II, III, VII, and VIII from a nine-poem
sequence called "Jottings from the Ragaz Churchyard."

On the Poet's Material

Muzot, from a letter to Countess Sizzo, March 17, 1922.

The first paragraph of the letter gives insight into the context of these reflections:

> *Château de Muzot sur Sierre,*
> *Valais (Switzerland),*
> *March 17, 1922*

My dear Countess,

The 17th ["a date of special meaning in the life of Countess Sizzo" according to the German editor] is too lovely a date for me not to feel tempted to set it at the head of a few pages, with which I hope I may reply to your gracious letter (which arrived yesterday). –All the more so in that my work, long and deeply interrupted, seems to have been saved – not only is it now here, but another small volume, *Sonnets* (the *Sonnets to Orpheus*), has been granted to me as a sort of additional gift in the unpredictable tempest of work. – But about the larger poems, yes, they are the ones begun in the winter of 1912 at Duino, then continued in Spain and Paris, until the war and the postwar period threatened to make it impossible – I have often had reason to fear – to finish them and give them their final shape. That would have been a hard blow, because these poems contain the most important, most valid truths that I have been able to discover in my middle years – , it would have been the bitterest twist of fate to be cut off at precisely the most mature inner place, to be prevented from bringing to completion that for which so many prerequisites of suffering and conjectures of bliss had laid the groundwork. These "Elegies" (that has been the title of these poems from the beginning – now there will be *ten* of them –) will now be preserved under the title *The Duino Elegies*, especially now that the time of war has destroyed the protective walls of this wonderful Adriatic castle (in whose hospitable solitude

the first two elegies came into existence, along with several fragments which now appear in the later poems), almost down to the last trace (: "Le buste survit à la cité," Théophile Gautier wrote, if memory serves, in one of his completed sonnets).

MARRIAGE
Meudon, early 1905.

Meudon was Rodin's country home, where Rilke was then living. See the Chronology for further information about Rilke's marriage.

IN HIS THIRTY-EIGHTH YEAR
From Rilke's diary, May 1, 1913.

Rilke was then thirty-seven, i.e., in his thirty-eighth year.

FROM TESTAMENT
Late April, 1921.

The strange document from which these passages are taken consists of a twelve-page introduction titled "Testament," written in the third person as though by a literary executor and describing the recent history of "the writer" whose papers this testament purports to be, wrapped around a fifty-page collection of fragments, notes, and drafts of letters which Rilke collected and titled, again, "Testament." Much of the introduction describes his despair during and after World War I; much of the rest concerns his love affair with Baladine Klossowska (mother of the writer Pierre Klossowska and the painter Balthus), or as he called her, "Merline." Selected here are only three of the items within the inner, framed "Testament."

"COME THEN, COME, YOU LAST THING I HAVE LEARNED"
Val-Mont, mid-December 1926.

Rilke died on December 29, 1926.

ON SHAWLS AND LEMONS (I)
Bern, October 1923. Unfinished.

On Shawls and Lemons (II)
Bern, October 1923. Unfinished.

On Shawls and Lemons (III)
Muzot, from a letter to Countess Sizzo, December 16, 1923.

On Shawls and Lemons (IV)
Ragaz, around July 1, 1924. Unfinished.

"There is total silence..."
Meudon (Rodin's home), fall 1906.

From the Notebooks (Naples)
Naples, shortly before mid-January 1907.
On the Lady and the Unicorn tapestries, see the note to "The Lady and the Unicorn" above. On his wife Clara Westhoff-Rilke, see the Chronology.

From the Notebooks (Capri)
Capri, January 24 or 25 and February 1, 1907.

From the Notebooks (Paris)
Paris, August 3 to early October 1907. These selections are scattered among others in the *Complete Works*; unlike the Naples and Capri sections, this is not a complete selection.

Night Songs (I)
Paris, June 1911. Unfinished.

Night Songs (II)
Worpswede, September 12, 1900.

Note on Birds
From a letter to Lou Andreas-Salomé, February 20, 1914, about her book *Three Letters to a Young Man*, which Rilke read in manuscript; this letter is quoted in a footnote of Salomé's in the

book itself (published in 1917). On Andreas-Salomé, see the Chronology.

SPRING SONGS (I): Early Spring
Muzot, February 20, 1924.

SPRING SONGS (II): Song for Helene
Letter to Helene Woronin, St. Petersburg, May 20, 1899.

"IT'S NOT THAT NOW THAT WE'RE (SUDDENLY) GROWN UP"
Vienna, early 1916.
    Unfinished; bracketed passages were crossed out by Rilke.

WHEN DEATH CAME WITH THE MORNING
From Rilke's diary, Worpswede, September 27, 1900.
    The image of roses as eyelids continued to preoccupy Rilke throughout his life. In his will, on October 27, 1925, he asked to have the following lines inscribed on his grave:

> Rose, oh pure contradiction, wanting
> to be Nobody's sleep under so many
> eyelids.

"LOOKING UP FROM THE BOOK, FROM THE NEAR AND COUNTABLE LINES"
Paris, February 1914.

DREAM (FRAGMENT)
Capri, February 1907.
    Unfinished; found in Rilke's papers in a manuscript titled "Dreams. 1902/1907" and also containing the first version of "The Twenty-Sixth Dream."

THE ORIGIN OF THE CHIMERA
Paris, summer 1908.

FROM THE DREAM-BOOK
Capri, early to mid-February 1907; planned since 1902; published in October 1907.

The seventh and eleventh dreams were probably drafted in 1902. The text is complete as is; Rilke assigned arbitrary dream numbers and put "From" in the title to emphasize its fragmentary character.

MORNING PRAYER
Written for morning prayers in Friedelhausen, August 1905.

"WHAT BIRDS HURTLE THROUGH IS NOT THE FAMILIAR SKY"
Muzot, June 16, 1924.

See the translator's afterword for an extended discussion of this poem.

INTRODUCTION TO A POETRY READING
Delivered October 27, 1919, in Zürich, upon Rilke's liberating escape from Germany and arrival in Switzerland.

Translator's Afterword

The contents of the book in your hand were not gathered together during Rilke's lifetime; it includes a mix of poetry and prose, with none of the *New Poems*, *Duino Elegies*, or *Sonnets to Orpheus*, and in fact almost nothing that Rilke published himself; the pieces are not in chronological order, nor collected around a single topic as in the many themed volumes there are in German: Rilke On Love, On Art, On Work, On Nature. Yet *The Inner Sky* makes a strong if implicit claim to be a whole, a coherent aspect of Rilke's creativity, not a grab-bag of scraps. In fact, it sets out to present a new Rilke in English, one a bit like the medieval saints and painters, or like Hopkins, or Dickinson: mystical via the concrete and visual, not abstract and philosophical. More than for most books, a detailed account of the translation and selection process can help to explain how this book came to be what it is.

　　The Inner Sky was born, that is to say conceived, on August 5, 2005. I was preparing to teach a translation-themed writing course and was rereading Anne Carson's miraculous book on love and consonants, *Eros the Bittersweet*, when I came across a chapter epigraph from Rilke: "Space reaches out from us and translates the world." I was intrigued and found the poem in my copy of Stephen Mitchell's *Selected Poetry of Rainer Maria Rilke*.

　　Mitchell's book was my initiation into poetry itself, as I think it was for many Americans roughly my age. I had since learned German, and Edward Snow's translation of Rilke's *New Poems* had helped convince me to pursue graduate school in literature, but I had not tried to translate any Rilke. I always had the same experience with bilingual editions of Rilke's poetry: after skimming through the German to see the basic sound and structure of the poem, I would slowly read the English, then look back at the German and it was as if the entire German language had been put together specifically so that this extraordinary construction of ideas and images would come out in beautifully rhymed and metered poetry. Again and again it was

simply astonishing that thoughts and feelings so original and complex could also be language so perfect.

Stephen Mitchell's translation of the epigraph line was "Space reaches *from* us and construes the world." When I looked across the spine at the German, I saw that Rilke had indeed written *übersetzt*, "translates"; Mitchell often shifts Rilke's terms into a more universal register, and maybe the poem was not about translation per se after all; anyway, space as translating the world doesn't seem to make much sense. But I was still under the spell of the day's Anne Carson, who tries to preserve strangeness in her translations: "Eros once again limb-loosener whirls me" is how she tends to put things (this is her translation of a line of Sappho). So "construes" was a bit disappointing, and a certain space for me to explore had opened up. Here is the poem in German and in Mitchell's translation:

> Durch den sich Vögel werfen, ist nicht der
> vertraute Raum, der die Gestalt dir steigert.
> (Im Freien, dorten, bist du dir verweigert
> und schwindest weiter ohne Wiederkehr.)
>
> Raum greift aus uns und übersetzt die Dinge:
> daß dir das Dasein eines Baums gelinge,
> wirf Innenraum um ihn, aus jenem Raum,
> der in dir west. Umgieb ihn mit Verhaltung.
> Er grenzt sich nicht. Erst in der Eingestaltung
> in dein Verzichten wird er wirklich Baum.
>
>   – Rainer Maria Rilke

> What birds plunge through is not the intimate space
> in which you see all forms intensified.
> (Out in the Open, you would be denied
> your self, would disappear into that vastness.)
>
> Space reaches *from* us and construes the world:
> to know a tree in its true element,

throw inner space around it, from that pure
abundance in you. Surround it with restraint.
It has no limits. Not till it is held
in your renouncing is it truly there.

– tr. Stephen Mitchell

What struck me next was in line 8: *Umgieb ihn mit Verhaltung*, translated as "Surround it with restraint." *Umgieb* is an odd word. It is the imperative of the verb *umgeben*, and German is a language with clear grammatical markers that comfortably makes words out of other words: *geben* means "give" and often "is" – *es gibt* ("it gives") is the way to say "there is" something – and *um* means "around." The normal word is *Umgebung*, a noun form of *umgeben*, which means surroundings or environment, i.e., *was es gibt um* (*dich*), what there is around (you). *Umgeben* is thus "to surround" in a descriptive, impersonal sense, the way a landscape "surrounds" you; there are other words for more actively surrounding enemy forces and so on. Rilke's *umgieb* wrenches this placid verb into an imperative: "Surround." *Verhaltung* is a noun form of the verb *verhalten*, which means to restrain, control, hold back, or curb something; the noun *Verhalten* means behavior, how you conduct yourself, as though acting properly were necessarily to control and restrain your urges. Other related words are *Verhaltensmassregeln*, or rules of conduct; *Verhaltung*'s only dictionary definition, which is the medical term for retaining water; and *Verhältnis*, a third noun form of *verhalten*, which means a relationship or relations with someone or something – as though that too were necessarily to hold something back – as well as "proportion" or "ratio" in the mathematical sense, among other meanings.

In any case, "Surround it with restraint" is a dull line of poetry. It means something interesting in the context of this poem, and Mitchell expressed that meaning but I wondered if it was possible to capture the strangeness too, especially the twisting of *Umgebung* into *umgieb*. And so the English word "environment" led to the unusual imperative "environ" – an almost exact match of the twist in German. All the *r*'s and *n*'s buzz

unpleasantly in "Environ it with restraint," and "restraint" is a bit stuffy, but maybe "Environ it with measure": "measure" is always an intriguing word to put into a poem because it invokes bars of music and thus the feet or meter of the poem itself.

The other flat moment in Mitchell immediately follows: "It has no limits," which is static and informational. The German again has more tension: *Es grenzt sich nicht. Grenze* is the word for border or frontier, often a very loaded word (for example in the work of Ingeborg Bachmann), and *grenzt* is the verb form, which would normally be used for "borders" in the static sense of "Arizona borders Mexico." Rilke uses *sich*, the reflexive pronoun, as the object of the verb; like *se* in French, the reflexive is much more common in German than in English, and is used in impersonal constructions: not just for phrases like "I wash myself" but, for example, "English is spoken here," which in French is *L'anglais se parle ici* ("English speaks itself here"). So "It has no limits" is perfectly correct for *Es grenzt sich nicht*, but the language is less active, and it doesn't make much sense to say that something has no limits if you have just environed or surrounded it with restraint or measure. Plus *Eros the Bittersweet* has several chapters on the metaphysics of the edge, and is filled with edgy translations, hence: "Environ it with measure. It will not edge itself." It is starting to sound like poetry again.

174

There are two things that happen at this stage of the translation process. The first is that I wonder what the rest of the poem would sound like if it were translated like this, or rather, what the rest of the poem would have to sound like in order to incorporate these two half-lines the way I had just translated them. I decide to keep going, to try to translate the poem. Secondly, these more vigorous, sharper-edged lines raise the big question more strongly than before: What is Rilke talking about? What does this poem actually mean? You read "Surround it with restraint. It has no limits" and you keep going; you read "Environ it with measure. It will not edge itself" and are brought up short.

To skip ahead for a moment, here is more or less what the poem means. The first stanza says that there is normal, everyday, external space, in which birds fly around and so on, and

then there's a space inside you; the outer environment is less familiar, more dangerous, you lose yourself out there. Rilke makes this point relatively often. The second stanza describes the two spaces in ways more particular to this poem: the idea is similar to the cliché that everyone sees things from their own perspective, but instead of the metaphor of "perspective," or angle of view, Rilke's metaphor is of an object and its background, or figure and ground in painting terms. He says that each of us takes our inner world and flings it out past whatever is out there so that it constitutes the background or negative space against which the object in the world is delimited. In this metaphor, what matters is not the angle you see from but the fact that things are undefined unless they stand out against something, and what they stand out against comes from inside you.

This is a strange idea to wrap your head around and is very interesting. The word *übersetzt* or "translates" gives it a nice touch too: "trans-late" in English is to carry across; *tra-duire* in French is to lead across; and *über-setzen* in German is to place across, or over, which is precisely what happens to this inner space vis-à-vis the things of the world. The space is put beyond or above the tree. "Space reaches out from us and trans-lates the world" makes more sense than it seemed to; and the German literally says "translates *things*," which is even clearer. You would almost wish that the German word for "translate" were *über-werfen*, "throw across" – and in fact, in a letter discussing André Gide, who had translated Rilke and whom Rilke had translated in the other direction, Rilke calls translation a *Hinüberwerfung* into the other language: a throwing of something over a wall or across a gap. (– Like so many major poets, Rilke was also a translator: he wrote a substantial amount of poetry in French at the end of his life, and his collected translations, from French, Italian, Latin, Middle High German, Flemish, English, Danish, Swedish, and Russian, fill close to 1,200 pages; an important but little-known essay on poetry translation makes the strong case that Rilke's translation of Valéry's "Le cimetière marin" is "one of the most successful poetic translations of our time" [John Frederick Nims, *Sappho to Valéry: Poems in Translation*, p. xxix].) In any case, Rilke's

poem about birds and inner space should be startling in English, and the images more sharply defined than in Mitchell, especially since that's what the poem is about.

There is one more word I need to discuss, because its translation was not only the breakthrough for this poem but launched the entire project of this book. That word is *Raum*, which appears four times in the poem and is absolutely key to its structure: it is the subject of the first sentence, the first word of stanza two, compounded with *Innen-* or "interior" in line 7, and the last word of line 7, rhyming with *Baum* or "tree," the last word in the poem. In a sense it rhymes with *Baum* twice, as the end-words of lines 7 and 10 and as the first and last words of stanza two, completing a circle. The rhyme is particularly crucial in this case because the whole argument of the poem is to describe how the inner world and the tree interact with each other, thus even though Mitchell's translation is loosely rhymed, he does not keep the most important rhyme in the poem. (Of course, cavilling about word choice in a rhymed translation is totally unfair, and I hope Mitchell will forgive me.)

The dictionary definition of *Raum* is "space," both outer space and space in the more abstract, Newtonian sense. The abstractness is the problem, because I could not keep the second stanza from sounding foggy with its talk of "space reaching out" and "inner space." (It is perhaps particular to my generation that "inner space" kept reminding me of *Inner Space*, the Dennis Quaid/Martin Short movie from the 1980s, but these considerations are part of the translation process too.) *Raum* in German is more concrete: it also means things like a room in a house, and "territory"; it's where the English word "room" comes from. Lastly, "space" doesn't rhyme with "tree." *Baum* could rather aggressively be translated as "spruce," but that would lose the tree's archetypal quality.

Puzzling through these issues, I ask myself what the "space" in lines 1–2 actually means. What is an intimate space that birds don't fly through? This is when I start to figure out the paraphrase of the poem that I gave earlier: that there are birds in the sky out there but another world inside you. Casual paraphrase

is always extraordinarily useful for finding clearer, more vivid language. So why not translate *Raum* as "sky," even though there is a different word for "sky" in German? A "space" is a zone, an abstraction, but a "sky" is a world – you read "inner sky" and you feel something vast open up inside you. There are birds in the sky, that makes perfect sense, but that's not the real sky, the sky you really know is the sky within. "Sky" also slant-rhymes with "tree," and "inner sky" solves the "inner space" problem, and I tried it and the poem came together.

Now *Raum* plays a significant role throughout Rilke's work. The word appears in five of the ten *Duino Elegies*, often in a context of birds, throwing, and interiority, for example: "Fling emptiness out of your arms / and into the skies we breathe; maybe then the birds will feel / a wider air with more intimate flight" (First Elegy, end of stanza 1). Critics have also focused on Rilke's concept of *Weltinnenraum*, the lyrical inner universe whose name Rilke coins by fusing the world (*Welt*) with the *Innenraum*, or infusing interiority into the *Weltraum* (literally "world-space" but this is the normal German word for "outer space"). (–And not only critics: At the climax of his great short novel *The Afternoon of a Writer*, Peter Handke asks "What was the business of a writer? Was there any such business in this century?... Who could claim to be an artist and lay claim to a *Weltinnenraum* in himself?" And then he answers.) We might translate *Weltinnenraum* with Hopkins's "inscape," or with something like this:

> Durch alle Wesen reicht der *eine* Raum:
> Weltinnenraum. Die Vögel fliegen still
> Durch uns hindurch. O, der ich wachsen will,
> Ich seh hinaus, und *in* mir wächst der Baum. . . .
>   – from "Es winkt zu Fühlung. . . "

> One single space extends through every being:
> An inniverse, the whole world's sky within.
> Birds fly in silence through us. O, the I

Who wants to grow looks out, and that is when
The tree grows *in* me. . . .

Lastly, I would mention that there are also birds in the Seventh
Elegy, whom the season of the year *wirft, in die innigen Himmel*
– "throws into the intimate sky." Rilke here uses *Himmel*, the dic-
tionary word for "sky."

For better or worse, I went with "sky" for *Raum* and shaped
a whole book around this one choice. Here, for comparison, are
my final translation, Stephen Mitchell's, and the translation by
the other major Rilke translator into English, Edward Snow.
I love Snow's translations too: as I mentioned earlier, his *New
Poems* was very important to me. He is best with the crystalline
structure of Rilke's concrete, precise poems; I do feel that in
poems like this one, where Rilke more sweepingly channels the
gods, Snow's literal translations sometimes fail to provide
enough grandeur.

> Durch den sich Vögel werfen, ist nicht der
> vertraute Raum, der die Gestalt dir steigert.
> (Im Freien, dorten, bist du dir verweigert
> und schwindest weiter ohne Wiederkehr.)
>
> Raum greift aus uns und übersetzt die Dinge:
> daß dir das Dasein eines Baums gelinge,
> wirf Innenraum um ihn, aus jenem Raum,
> der in dir west. Umgieb ihn mit Verhaltung.
> Er grenzt sich nicht. Erst in der Eingestaltung
> in dein Verzichten wird er wirklich Baum.
>   – Rainer Maria Rilke

> What birds plunge through is not the intimate space
> in which you see all forms intensified.
> (Out in the Open, you would be denied
> your self, would disappear into that vastness.)

Space reaches *from* us and construes the world:
to know a tree in its true element,
throw inner space around it, from that pure
abundance in you. Surround it with restraint.
It has no limits. Not till it is held
in your renouncing is it truly there.

– tr. Stephen Mitchell

What birds plunge through is not that intimate space
in which you feel all forms intensified.
(There, in the Open, you'd be denied yourself
and vanish on and on without return.)

Space reaches out from us and translates each thing:
to accomplish a tree's essence
cast inner space around it, out of that space
that has its life in you. Surround it with restraint.
In itself it has no bounds. Only in the spell
of your renouncing does it rise as Tree.

– tr. Edward Snow

What birds hurtle through is not the familiar sky
that raises form and shape within you.
(Out in the open, out there, you are denied
to yourself and fade, fade farther, forever.)

Sky grabs out from us and translates things:
that you might reach a tree in all its being
fling inner sky around it, from that sky
that abides in you. Ring it with measure.
It will not edge itself. Only the pressure
in your renouncing makes it truly tree.

– tr. Damion Searls

Notice for *umgieb*, the first word I translated, the clever solution I was so proud of did not make it into the final version. That happens sometimes. I went with "ring" instead of "environ" partly for visual clarity and partly to rhyme with "fling" and "thing" and "being" in that passage of heavy assonance, "sky" and "abides" and "might," "reach a tree in all its being." (The German is downright outrageous: *dass dir das Dasein*; *Innenraum um ihn*.) The word *umgieb* drew my attention to Rilke's vigorous, unusual language, but brought me to a sense of the poem where concrete imagery would always outweigh baroque or abstract vocabulary.

I will not go through the rest of the poem in such detail, but "fling" in line 7 is worth mentioning – I was going for vigor, as with "grabs" in line 5, but the word is something of a failure because it translates *wirf* ("throw"), the same verb as *werfen* in line 1. The birds *werfen sich* or "throw themselves / are thrown" through the sky, in the reflexive construction I discussed above. But birds "throwing themselves around" doesn't mean the same thing in English; I used "hurtle" right up against "birds" to capture more of Rilke's play with sound, and in any case the vowels and consonants of "throw" in line 7 would sound wrong in my translation (Mitchell makes it work by putting "know" in line 6, but "know" is too cognitive for how I see the poem). Hence the failure of "fling," which has no connection with the word "hurtle": it is too bad to lose the link in the original, the argument that you throw your inner sky but birds, in the same act, throw themselves – that birds are their own sky.

This line of thought reminded me of another Rilke poem about throwing and catching, which I knew because its first half is the epigraph to Hans-Georg Gadamer's *Truth and Method*, the subject of my undergraduate thesis many years ago. I had to use a Rilke concordance and look up forms of "throw" to find it, and when I did I was surprised to see that the poem, "As long as you catch what you've thrown yourself," was also about birds and was in all sorts of ways a perfect companion to the poem I had just translated. The last word of the poem is *Räume*, the plural of *Raum*: what would it sound like to translate the

word as "skies" there too? It turns out the imagery becomes much more concrete and visual; see what is now the first poem in this book. I will not reproduce Snow's translation here for comparison (Rilke, *Uncollected Poems*, 1996, p. 139), but it ends "Out of your hands the meteor / would launch itself and flame into its spaces," and I don't think that works as culminating lines of poetry. After translating the poem myself, I now see it as Rilke's special effects spectacular: the poet stands, superhero-like, with an impassively upturned hand, and an orb appears a few inches above his palm, spinning slightly, gently glowing. You hear a high-pitched hum, or whine, and the ball ignites; orange flames lick around it; then, without any visible motion from the poet, there is a deafening whoosh of surround sound, and it rockets into outer space.

At this point I realized that I had something on my hands too: a vision of translating Rilke which could stand beside Mitchell's vatic mysticism and Snow's precision as another important voice for Rilke in English. This Rilke, described in the first paragraph of the present afterword, is one I had experienced but had never seen foregrounded or "edged" before. I could select the writings of Rilke that exemplified this side of him and translate them in a way that expressed it, or select the writings that *could* be translated this way: the selection and translation of *The Inner Sky: Poems, Notes, Dreams* were really two sides of the same process. For example, the connection lost between flinging your inner sky and the birds hurling themselves through space could be recaptured by including the other poem about birds and throwing, as well as the "Note on Birds," in which Rilke says more about why birds are their inner skies. "Notes on the Melody of Things," where Rilke starts from the gold background that Italian painters put behind their saints, is part of what borders and defines the inner sky poem, as is the description of the village girls in his Czech homeland in "Interiors," where he says that he cannot help but "imagine an ocean behind them, or a grave eternal plain, or something else you don't actually see with your eyes but can only sense." I translated consistently across the different pieces, for instance

using "sky" for *Raum* wherever possible (I couldn't force it into, e.g., the "interior space" of the garden passageway in "On Shawls and Lemons III"); I even translated *bras d'espace* from French (in "Night Songs I") as "arms of sky," not "arms of space" – not just for consistency, but also, again, for concreteness and visual clarity.

I used the concordance to find more poems about "throwing," and poems with other key words, like *Raum*; certain themes and motifs started to emerge, like foreground and background, activity and passivity, and Rilke's imagining himself to be a girl or a woman, and these thematic centers drew new pieces to them like the center of a nebula slowly forming itself. The weakness of a translation style aiming for concrete simplicity is that my versions sometimes sounded too simplistic; admittedly, too, some of Rilke's poems are just not as good as the rest, or repeat other poems on similar themes. These were omitted. The order of the selections took shape as intuitively as any of the translations – for translation is an intuitive process, even if I have slowed it down in this afterword and made it seem more analytical than it is. I am not a Rilke scholar, I have not read everything Rilke wrote, certainly not all his letters or manuscripts, but the inner sky of my vision reached out and translated the mass of Rilke's complete works into a defined and bordered tree with a coherent form and shape, not my shape but its shape, edged by me but truly its own.

Lastly, I noticed I was selecting and translating the kind of poetry and prose that Rilke tended not to publish, and a sort of rule developed not to include any of the poems Rilke collected into his own books. I started to feel that the pieces in *The Inner Sky* capture a personal, vulnerable side of Rilke that he typically tried to suppress or repress in his magisterial book-personas. This book is not, in other words, the whole Rilke, but it is an important side of the whole Rilke, one which has hitherto been hard to see in English. Robert Hass's great essay "Looking for Rilke," the introduction to Mitchell's *Selected Poetry of Rainer Maria Rilke*, emphasizes that "of all poets, Rilke is the hardest to locate in a place," that in fact he is placeless: "Rilke's special

gift as a poet is that he does not seem to speak from the middle of life, that he is always calling us away from it" (pp. xiii, xiv). After the autobiographical prose pieces in *The Inner Sky* – "Interiors," "In His Thirty-Eighth Year," "From Testament," and others – that doesn't seem quite right. The Rilke in this book speaks from right in our midst, even if in a voice from somewhere else: he is "channeling the gods," as I put it earlier.

"As long as you catch what you've thrown yourself" is among other things a poem about translation, about catching a ball and throwing it back, which is what translators do in their reading and *Hinüberwerfung*. It is also a model of creativity. As I mention in my Notes, a section where I included various pieces that didn't belong in the book proper, this poem was written just two days before the legendary burst of creativity, or receptivity, that produced all of the *Sonnets to Orpheus* and half of the *Duino Elegies* in three weeks. I know people who wonder what it must have been like to be Rilke during those three weeks, but I wonder more about the days of prelude. How could he possibly have gotten to sleep on the two nights after he wrote this poem, when he must have known that his years and years of waiting were near an end? He felt the forces gathering in his inner sky, about to burst forth like a star, and it is characteristic of Rilke that he felt these forces as a gift from something external to where we are, something eternal – felt them as a poem to catch, to translate.

Envoi:
Introduction to a Poetry Reading
Hottingen Book Club, Zürich

The kind invitation of the H.B.C.,
which I am finally able to accept,
has prompted me – after a very long hiatus – to resume giving
public readings.
    I thank you in advance, that you: the Swiss
would like to be the first to listen to my poetry (again).
    When I gave up giving poetry readings – it must have been
ten years ago now – I did so under the impression that a poem
. . . makes its appeal to a

$$\left.\begin{array}{l} \text{too narrow} \\[1em] \text{limited} \end{array}\right\} \text{immediate}$$

sense of community for it to be able to be trotted out just like
that before a multitude of people.
    If I were to step before an audience again, I thought, it
would have to be to give a talk, for a talk is, by its very nature, a
communication from one place to another – ; whereas I will have
several poems to present today that may seem to you (there is
no help for it) truly lacking their prerequisites; they may seem
inconsiderate, or merciless; if, that is, you don't simply (to an-
ticipate the worst case) lose patience and take them to be a kind
of *poésie de luxe*.

The question of how much patience to grant to a work of art
that appears before you like this, without an agenda – especially
in these times, which are in such desperate need of advice – and
whether, in the end, it isn't to be received as some kind of aid
or support from the farthest, outermost distance, as a word of
comfort with a coefficient of *infinity* – ; I hope you will let me
refrain from posing this question today.

184

It would create an atmosphere of discussion or debate between us, which is not the atmosphere that should bind us together this evening.

Allow me to state only this much:

It did not require the horrific last few years to make me examine whether the bringing forth of such things is responsible or not.

Almost twenty years ago, walking with Leo Tolstoy through the fields of forget-me-nots at Yasnaya Polyana, I already had to make this fundamental decision.

Since then, I don't know how often, at every turn in my path, I have called my own activity into question, treated it as a heavy, difficult burden, and have tested myself and beset myself with the question of whether this activity truly passes the test, whether I truly pass the test.

Who can affirm anything of the future?
but until now, the answering inner voice has always continued to approve.

*

These works, some of which I may present to you tonight, in some way arise from the conviction that it is a legitimate, particular task to bring forth pure evidence of the breadth,
    diversity,
        even fullness and completion of the world.

Yes! I have hoped to rear each poem into a witness that would be able to understand everything for me,
every appearance,
        not only emotional things,
lyrically: – to present
    an animal,
        a plant,
            every event,
                a thing
in its proper space of feeling.

Do not let yourself be put off by the fact that I often call up images of the past. That which was also is, in the fullness of occurring, if you grasp it not according to its content but by means of its intensity. And we – as members of a world which brings forth movement after movement, force after force, seeming to crash into inexorably fewer and fewer visible objects – we have to rely on this superior visibility of the past if we want to represent, in allegorical form, the hidden splendor of the present which we are surrounded by even today.

I will not bury you in a mountain of utterances tonight. I promise to be economical.

I have not decided in advance which pieces to read.

I intend to choose this or that poem under the influence of your presence and your participation.

As a result, I hope you will also have patience for my occasionally being prompted to insert a few short remarks, and so, as the case arises, to create a platform on which you can assemble and observe.

In all of this, I feel less like someone trying to call forth pleasure from you –

what I ask of you is this:

let us, as far as possible, do everything we can for the true, honest community of this

hour!

Index of English Titles and First Lines

After a great strain, like my production of work last year, 37

All of the flags are held up higher, 113

Among her twenty jars of make-up, 65

And in autumn to understand the gray, 113

As bliss takes shelter here, so worked in, 101

As, for the virgin, from he who kneels before her, 93

As long as you catch what you've thrown yourself, 9

As though all my hard childhood, 111

Autumn Evening, 111

A young girl: she is like a star, 31

Butterfly the wind has tossed, 67

Come then, come, you last thing I have learned, 91

Day of pain that gapes like a wound, 11

Dedication, 41

Describe the vineyards at the moment when, on a windy day, 109

Do not think, artist, that work is what tests you, 83

Dream, 131

Early Spring, 119

Feast of the Dead, 67

From Testament, 83

From the Dream-Book, 135

From the Notebooks, 107

Haiku, 65

Hardness has vanished. Suddenly solace, 119

How much time it has taken him to see through his oldest, 79

I am an image, 164

I can imagine no knowledge holier, 45

In His Thirty-Eighth Year, 79

Interiors, 13

In the Naples museum, we stood for a long while, 107

Introduction to a Poetry Reading, 184

I observed it first in military school, 83

It confuses us, we for whom being means, 111

It's not that now that we're (suddenly) grown up, 121

I've discovered a new caress, 125

I've figured it out, something that was never clear, 117

I was looking for the young girl, 135

Lady, Your Ladyship – : how we must wound, 33

Let nothing be preserved of that difficult, "alien" disaster, 85

Looking up from the book, from the near and countable lines, 129

Look – night is opening her arms of sky to you, 115

Marriage, 77

Maybe it was always that way, 35

Morning Prayer, 149

Naturally, it makes sense to send your song aloft, 75

Night Songs, 115

(Nonexistent) Child's Grave with Ball, 69

Note on Birds, 117

Notes on the Melody of Things, 45

Not one of these crosses, nor all, 69

O flight from us and flight into the shawl, 93

On Completing the Circle, 35

On Shawls and Lemons, 93
On the Poet's Material, 75
On work days arise to your labors
    happily, if you can, 149
Our doors shut tight, 67
Our greatest task is this, 41
Poems from the Graveyard, 67
Pregnant Woman, 11
Rose, oh pure contradiction, 169
She is sad, wordless and alone, 77
Silver Pleasure Roughness Rounded
    Lot Lover, 87
Song for Helene, 119
Spring Songs, 119
Still, fruits are much heavier than
    flowers, 65
That game where you stand against a
    tree, 73
The dead man was extraordinarily
    big, 131
The kind invitation of the H.B.C.,
    184
The Lady and the Unicorn, 33
The ocean, under a close gray sky,
    109
The Origin of the Chimera, 133
There are tapestries here, Abelone,
    tapestries on the wall, 160
There is total silence, upright in
    overgrown, 105

The wells in the Certosa di San
    Martino, 107
The youngest angel, his ready too-
    sweet, 133
Vitali Awoke, 43
We all need warm rains like the one
    that's been, 119
We are right at the start, do you see, 45
We take this thing that belongs to us
    and throw it, 71
What birds hurtle through is not the
    familiar sky, 153
What I want on stage, in the space
    above, 165
When Death Came with the
    Morning, 125
When the feeling of one of the
    distant cities, 113
Wind from the moon, 111
With all my abundances I bless you,
    115
Works of Art, 35
Yes, I know Weltrus Park, 93
You know how the shimmer of light
    falls through the leaves, 69
You must have seen them: these
    small towns, 13
Young Girl, 31
You were in a position to throw and
    you threw, 71

Index of Original Titles and First Lines

Alle Fahnen sind höher hinauf-
gehalten, 112

Als der Tod mit dem Morgen kam,
124

Als wäre meine schwere, 110

À Mademoiselle Sophy Giauque,
40

[Aufzeichnung], 78

[Aufzeichnungen aus Neapel und
Capri], 106

Aus dem Traum-Buch, 134

C'est notre extrême labeur, 40

C'est pourtant plus lourd de porter
des fruits que des fleurs, 64

Das Meer unter nahem grauem
Himmel in drei Streifen, 108

Das (nicht vorhandene) Kindergrab
mit dem Ball, 68

Daß einer auf seinem angeborenen
Platz aufsänge, 74

Das Spiel, da man sich an die Bäume
stellt, 72

Das Testament, 82

Der Engel jüngster, als sein über-
süßer, 132

Der Ursprung der Chimäre, 132

Der Verstorbene war ein außer-
ordentlich großer, langer, hagerer
Mann, 130

Die Brunnen in der Certosa, 106

Durch den sich Vögel werfen, ist
nicht der, 152

Du warsts imstand und warfst ihn
weit hinein, 70

Ehe, 76

[Eine Morgenandacht], 148

Ein junges Mädchen: das ist wie ein
Stern, 30

Entre ses vingt fards, 64

[Entwürfe], 110

Es ist ganz stille. Aufrecht steht der
Duft, 104

Falter, über die Kirchhof-Mauer, 66

Frau und Erlauchte: sicher kränken
wir, 32

Ganz am Anfang sind wir, siehst du,
44

Glaube nicht, Künstler, daß deine
Prüfung in der Arbeit sei, 82

[Haï-Kaï], 64

Härte schwand. Auf einmal legt sich
Schonung, 118

Hebend die Blicke vom Buch, von
den nahen zählbaren Zeilen, 128

Herbst-Abend, 110

Ich erfand mir eine neue
Zärtlichkeit, 124

Ich kann mir kein seligeres Wissen
denken, 44

Ich segne dich mit meinen
Überflüssen, 114

Ich suchte das junge Mädchen, 134

Ihr genauer Bericht über Weltrus,
92

Im Kirchhof zu Ragaz
Niedergeschriebenes, 66

Im Museum von Neapel standen wir
lange, 106

In der Militärschule sah ich es zuerst
ein, 82

Intérieurs, 12

Kennst du das, daß durch das
Laubwerk Scheine, 68

Komm du, du letzter, den ich
anerkenne, 90

Kunstwerke, 34

La Dame à la Licorne, 32

Lied für Helene, 118

Man muß sie gesehen haben, diese
kleinen und ganz kleinen Städte, 12

189

Nach den großen Anstrengungen des vorigen Jahrs, 36

Nicht daß uns, da wir (plötzlich) erwachsen sind, 120

Nichts soll aus jener schweren ›fremden‹ Heimsuchung, 84

Notizen zur Melodie der Dinge, 44

O Flucht aus uns und Zu-Flucht in den Shawl, 92

Schön hab ichs aufgefaßt, wie mirs noch nie sich darstellte, 116

[Schwangere], 10

Shawl, 92, 100

Sie ist traurig, lautlos und allein, 76

Silber Freude Rohheit Runde Loos Lieber, 86

Solang du Selbstgeworfnes fängst, ist alles, 8

Sprich von den Weinbergen zur Zeit, da an einem windigen Tag, 108

Steh froh auf zu deinem Werktage, wenn du es kannst, 148

Toten-Mahl, 66

Träume [Bruchstück], 130

Und im Herbst der welkenden Façaden, 112

Unsere Türen schließen sehr fest, 66

Uns verwirrt es, die wir seiend heißen, 110

Vielleicht war es immer so, 34

Vitali erwachte, 42

Voilà la nuit t'ouvrant ses bras d'espace, 114

Von diesen Kreuzen keins, 68

Vorfrühling, 118

Wehtag, der wie eine Wunde klafft, 10

Wenn das Gefühl einer der fernen Städte, 112

Wie, für die Jungfrau, dem, der vor ihr kniet, die Namen, 92

Wie Seligkeit in diesem sich verbirgt, 100

Wieviel Zeit hatte er gebraucht, um seinen ältesten, verhängnisvollsten Fehler einzusehen, 78

Wind aus dem Mond, 110

Wir alle brauchen solchen warmen Regen, 118

Wir werfen dieses Ding, das uns gehört, 70

ABOUT THE AUTHOR

Rainer Maria Rilke, born on December 4, 1875, in Prague, was the greatest and best-loved European poet of the twentieth century. His major works include New Poems, Requiem *(for Paula Modersohn-Becker),* Duino Elegies, *and* The Sonnets to Orpheus, *and, in prose,* Letters to a Young Poet, Letters on Cézanne, *and the novel* The Notebooks of Malte Laurids Brigge. *He settled in Switzerland after World War I and died there on December 29, 1926.*

ABOUT THE TRANSLATOR

Damion Searls is the author of Everything You Say Is True, *a travelogue, and* What We Were Doing and Where We Were Going, *stories (Dalkey Archive, 2009). His translations include Marcel Proust's* On Reading, *Nescio's* Amsterdam Stories, *and a forthcoming retranslation of Hermann Hesse's* Demian; *his translation of Hans Keilson's* Comedy in a Minor Key *was a* New York Times *Notable Book of 2010, a National Book Critics Circle Award finalist, and won the 2011 Schlegel-Tieck Translation Prize. He lives in New York City with his wife and son.*